SECRET
AMSTERDAM

Marjolijn van Eys and Delphine Robiot
Photos Lynn van der Velden-Elliott
Translation Guy Roberts

Jonglez Publishing

We have taken great pleasure in drawing up
Secret Amsterdam and hope that through
its guidance you will, like us, continue to discover
unusual, hidden or little-known aspects of the city.
Descriptions of certain places are accompanied
by thematic sections highlighting historical details
or anecdotes as an aid to understanding the city
in all its complexity.
Secret Amsterdam also draws attention to
the multitude of details found in places that we
may pass every day without noticing. These are
an invitation to look more closely at the urban
landscape and, more generally, a means of seeing
our own city with the curiosity and attention that
we often display while travelling elsewhere…

Comments on this guidebook and its contents,
as well as information on places we may not have
mentioned, are more than welcome and will
enrich future editions.

Don't hesitate to contact us:
• Jonglez publishing, 17, boulevard du Roi,
  78000 Versailles, France.
• E-mail : info@jonglezpublishing.com

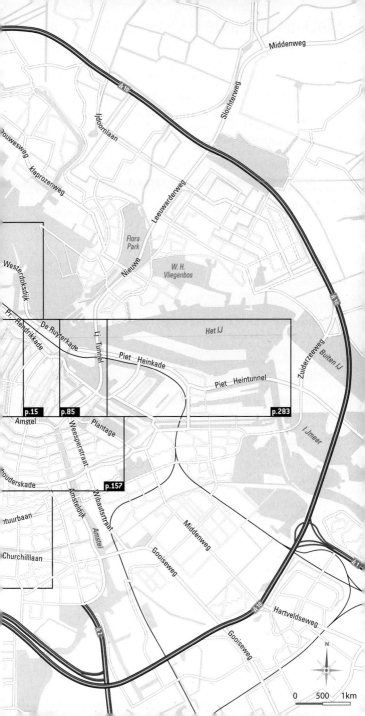

TABLE OF CONTENTS

NORTHWEST RING CANALS - JORDAAN

TABLE OF CONTENTS

TABLE OF CONTENTS

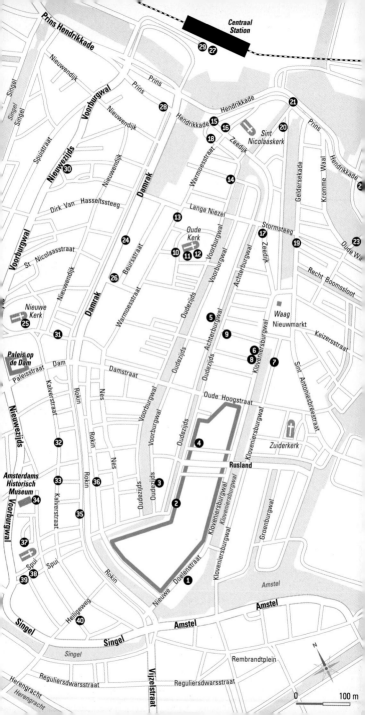

THE CENTRE

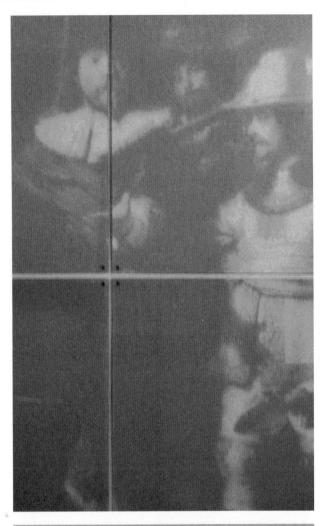

The "*Compagnie van Frans Banning Cocq*", the original name of the painting, was called the Civic Guard of the "Kloveniers", or arquebus gunners,
from the name of the weapon they used in the 16th century. In the painting one can see an arquebus gunner in the act of charging his weapon
with powder. One can also see, in the centre, a small girl carrying a
chicken upside down: its feet are very prominent. The name "Klauw",
which means claw, is a homonym of "Klove", meaning the arquebus. So,
the presence of the chicken is a symbolic reference to the Company.
The street extending beyond the Doelen is called "Kloveniersburgwal".

THE HISTORIC LOCATION
OF REMBRANDT'S FAMOUS NIGHT WATCH

❶

Hotel de Doelen
Nieuwe Doelenstraat 24, 1012CP Amsterdam
• Open daily

*Painted
for
a guard tower*

Between the Nieuwe Doelenstraat and the Kloveniersburgwal, on the north side of the building, is a decorative plaque, sculpted in 1883 by J.H. Teixeira de Mattos. It depicts the 'Doelen' as it was before being rebuilt in the 19th century; a fortified tower adjoining the headquarters and shooting range of one of Amsterdam's companies, the "Kloveniers". It was for the adornment of this building that Rembrandt's famous canvas "The Night Watch" was commissioned.

The tower was built in 1492 and originally known as "Swych Utrecht" (Silence Utrecht). It formed part of the city's fortifications, protecting it against attack from the southeast and its archenemy, Utrecht. It subsequently provided a meeting and exercising venue for the civic guard, known as the "Kloveniers", so-called after their weaponry, the 'Klover', an early firearm, later to be replaced by the musket.

In 1638, Captain Frans Banning Cocq asked Rembrandt to paint the company's portrait, an enormous task, which took him 4 years to complete. It was then hung in the great hall of the Doelen, alongside other portraits painted by Rembrandt's fellow artists, where it remained until 1715.

By this time, the Doelen had lost its military function and served as a banqueting hall and accommodation for Amsterdam's official guests. Hence Rembrandt's painting was moved to the city hall, and not being highly regarded, the canvas was trimmed both vertically and horizontally to fit it into a space above a chimney.

In 1870, J.F. Hahn purchased the Doelen and, anticipating the forthcoming Universal Exhibition of 1883 (see page 213), he had it rebuilt in neo-Renaissance style, at the same time demolishing the tower.

Fortunately, the rebuilding preserved the wall of the Doelen's great hall, where Rembrandt's painting formerly hung. Two statues depicting civic guards, also by J.H. Teixeira de Mattos, adorn the dome on the Amstel side of the hotel, recalling the location's military past. One of the musketeers is said to represent Rembrandt.

To view the interior, after having gained permission from the hotel's reception, take the staircase to the first floor and enter the corridor leading to rooms, 101-109. At the far end, a reproduction of Rembrandt's "Nightwatch" adorns the very wall, where the original once hung.

© The Hebrew University of Jerusalem & The Jewish National & University Library

THE REMAINS OF THE MEDIEVAL TOWN

The fortifications of the medieval town of Amsterdam were constructed between 1481 and 1494. Amsterdam was by then a prosperous commercial town and as such a possible target of assailants, especially as it had no natural defences.

Maximilian I of Austria, Regent of The Netherlands following the death of his wife Marie de Bourgogne in 1482, therefore decided to build ramparts around the town to protect it.

The fortifications consisted of surrounding walls built with bricks on a stone foundation, gates and towers. Hardly any vestiges remain from this era: only certain gates have been preserved and renovated.

The Geldersekade, is a very old Amsterdam quay, dating from the 15th Century, on which the defensive wall was built. One can still see a few sandstone relics of the wall between Nos 18 and 50. Lean carefully over the edge of the quay to see these pale-coloured stones.

VISIBLE REMAINS OF THE WALL OF THE MEDIEVAL TOWN

Schreierstoren
Sint Antoniespoort
Sint Olofspoort
Geldersekade: between Nos 18 and 50
Montelbaanstoren
Utrechtsepoort
Regulierspoort – Munttoren
Heiligewegspoort currently Heiligeweg
Haarlemmerpoort, moved several times and rebuilt in the 19th century

THE TRUE HISTORY OF THE ARMS OF THE TOWN OF AMSTERDAM

One could easily take the Arms of Amsterdam for a recent logo, so timeless is their design; however, they date from before 1505. The coat of arms comprises a red background across which extends a black vertical band enclosing three St Andrew's crosses. As Jesus' first disciple, St Andrew was very popular in the Middle Ages. He died a martyr, executed on a cross in the form of an X, to which he thus gave his name.

The black vertical band is supposed to represent the Amstel river, alongside which stretches the town of Amsterdam. Other Dutch towns built alongside rivers, like Dordrecht or Delft, also have a band in their arms.

The crosses, either white or silver-coloured, most likely derive from the arms of Jan van Persijn, Lord of Waterland of Aemstelle.

St Andrew may well have been one of Persijn's favourite Saints, as one finds these crosses in the arms of several towns older than Amsterdam, of which he was also Lord: Ouderkerk, with its 5 crosses on two horizontal bands and Amstelveen, with its 4 crosses on two black horizontal bands.

The crosses are also considered to symbolize the three great dangers faced by Amsterdam: water, fire and the plague.

After the Second World War, Queen Wilhelmina decided to denote an additional meaning to the crosses, in homage to the attitude of the people of Amsterdam during the war: heroism, determination and charity.

Since the 16th century, the arms of the town have been surmounted by a crown, which can also be seen on numerous monuments, churches or towers. It was Emperor Maximilian the First who authorized the town to use the imperial crown in 1489 (see page 67). This crown was much more than a decorative ornament.

It was an additional credibility for navigators, who mounted it proudly on the flags of their merchant ships.

THE SPECTACLES ABOVE THE PASSAGE ❷
OF THE OUDEMANSHUISPOORT
Oudezijds Achterburgwal 227, 1012DL Amsterdam
Kloveniersburgwal 80, 1012CZ Amsterdam
• Open Monday to Saturday from 11am to 5pm. In practice, the shops
often open later and close earlier, depending
on the whims of the booksellers

A door closes both ends of the book-sellers' passage, which once led to a hospice for the elderly poor, built at the beginning of the 17th century. In 1876, this building became part of the University of Amsterdam and today houses the Faculty of Law, but the passage itself still remains a place of commerce.

An ancient passage leading to a hospice for the elderly

In 1601, the building was constructed on the remains of the old convent of the nuns, known also as "the convent of the 11,000 virgins", which was deserted after the 'Alteration' (see page 25).

On the Oudezijds Achterburgwal side, a plaque above the door's Ionic columns depicts a pair of spectacles; in the 17th.century, a symbol of old age and referring to its earlier function as a home for Amsterdam's elderly paupers.

Construction of the building was financed with the proceeds from a lottery held in 1600 and, in 1616, a second lottery financed enlargement of the hospice. Above the door on the Kloveniersburgwal side, is a gable stone sculpted by Zieseniss in 1757; it depicts a woman with a horn of plenty, surrounded on both sides by old men, again symbolizing old age.

WHY ARE THE ARCADES EQUIPPED WITH HEAVY PROTECTIVE SHUTTERS ?
Opened in 1757, the 18 shops in the gallery were initially engaged trading gold and silver, hence every arcade was equipped with heavy shutters to prevent theft.
Today, they house the second-hand booksellers who were obliged to leave the Botermarkt, now the Rembrandtplein, in the middle of the 19th century.

THE ANCESTOR OF THE UNIVERSITY: THE ILLUSTRIOUS ATHENAEUM
The organization called the Illustrious Athenaeum was founded in January 1632, which is recorded in The Netherlands as the date of the establishment of the University.
Two famous professors from Leiden, who already enjoyed international renown, started teaching in the Chapel of Saint Agnes (see next page): Caspar Barlaeus, mathematician, poet and physician, and Gerardus Vossius, theologian. Their busts are located on the pretty square in front of the building.
The Illustrious Athenaeum's vocation was to provide education in commerce and philosophy. In 1815, it was officially recognized as an institute of higher education and, in 1877, reorganised to become the University of Amsterdam.

THE HISTORY OF THE PURPERHOEDENVEEM.

A "veem" is an old Dutch word for a kind of warehouse where a single product was stored, like cheese or tobacco.

The goods were brought there from a market by porters, who wore hats in the colour of their particular warehouses, to avoid confusion. In this case, the colour was "purper" (purple). This custom can still be observed in the re-enactment of the cheese market at Alkmaar.

DOORWAY AND CHAPEL OF SAINT AGNES ❸

Agnieten Kapel, Oudezijds Voorburgwal 231, 1012EZ Amsterdam
• Visit on request by phoning 020 525 28 08

The cradle of Amsterdam University

A vestige of the Middle Ages and cradle of Amsterdam University, the Chapel of Saint Agnes has succeeded in retaining its medieval character despite successive renovations. A visit, by appointment only, is well worthwhile.

The chapel originally belonged to the convent of the same name, founded by the Clarisse sisterhood on Saint Agnes Day, 21 January 1397.

Both the convent's original cloister and chapel, built of wood, were totally destroyed in Amsterdam's great fire of 1452. Subsequently, timber constructions were officially banned and the chapel was rebuilt in brick in 1470, in the Gothic style typical of that period.

In 1578, Amsterdam having become Protestant, the Catholic's churches and convents were closed.

Whilst, initially, its 30 nuns were allowed to continue living in the convent, whilst its chapel was taken over for use as an Admiralty storehouse.

In 1632, the chapel became the seat of the Illustrious Athenaeum, founded by the famous Leiden professors, Barlaeus and Vossius (see page 19).

An important centre of learning and forerunner of Amsterdam's University, in the 17th century, its loft also housed a public library. Hence, the chapel was restored and its original gateway replaced by one formerly providing entry to city's carpentry yard in the Nieuwe Doelenstraat. This gate, originally dating from 1571, was newly inscribed with the date of the chapel's restoration, 1631.

Today, the chapel is the only part of the convent to have been preserved and was again restored in 1921, when it was given a more traditional look, including, notably, the installation of the stained glass windows depicting Vossius and Barlaeus.

The most recent renovation, completed in early 2007, has applied a functional touch, by linking the building to the neighbouring Purperhoedenveem (see opposite page), which provides accommodation for events and congresses.

The renovation, however, has retained traces of the building's past, like the painted ceilings of the corridors. The great hall still continues to house a collection of paintings, donated in 1743 by the merchant Gerardus van Papenbroeck, depicting the great humanists: Erasmus, Hugo Grotius, Luther, Descartes and… Machiavelli.

From the opposite side of the Oudezijds Achterburgwal, one can observe the chapel's little bell tower.

TO SEE NEARBY

THE DOORWAY OF THE SPINHUIS PRISON
Spinhuissteeg 1, 1012DK Amsterdam

Until 1578, the convent of Saint Ursula stood on the land between the Spinhuissteeg and Korte Spinhuissteeg alleyways. The Spinhuis (spinning house) was built there in 1597. Here were imprisoned female beggars and prostitutes who were condemned to spin wool and undertake needlework.

In 1645, the building was reconstructed following a fire. The doorway on Spinhuissteeg is attributed to Hendrick de Keyser. Above the door is a fine high-relief depicting two tortured women. The evocative caption is a quotation from the famous poet of the 17th century, Pieter Cornelisz. Hooft, seeking to reassure passers-by: "Don't fear my vengeance, I undertake to be good. I have brought punishment on myself but my soul is pure". Today the Spinhuis houses the Social Sciences and Behaviour Faculty of Amsterdam University.

WHEN THIEVES, NAILED BY ONE EAR, COULD ONLY FREE THEMSELVES BY TEARING AWAY...

In the 16th and 17th centuries, punishments for beggars, imposters, thieves and prostitutes were incredibly cruel and severe. Criminals were put in a revolving cage for a quarter of an hour, and prostitutes exposed to public revenge. Thieves were nailed by one ear to a wall; they could only liberate themselves by tearing free. Whipping, branding with red-hot irons and severing of a hand were among the less severe punishments. As for beggars and vagabonds, they were simply banished from the town. Many finished up at the gallows, situated on the other side of the river IJ, in the present district of Volewijck (see bottom right on the map, page 16). The theologian, scholar and humanist Dirk Volkertsz. Coornhert (1522-1590) wrote a treatise in 1567 entitled "Boeventucht" or "discipline for miscreants", pleading for a different approach to imprisonment. In his opinion, prisoners should be put to work in houses of correction or on public projects, like digging canals or constructing dikes.

Following the paper's publication, two houses of correction, based on rehabilitation through work, were established in Amsterdam, the Rasphuis and the Spinhuis. Starting in 1603, a section combining a school and a house of correction was also established within the Spinhuis; youngsters with problems were sent there by their parents or their teacher to learn a suitable trade, thanks to which they could one day earn their living. On Sundays and winter evenings, they had lessons in reading and writing, as well as religious education.

The founding of the Rasphuis (see page 81) marked a significant change in judicial thinking, with resulting implications in other European countries.

The Coornhertliga or Coornhert League, a transnational jurists' association founded in 1971, took over this name and continues today to influence legislation on prison sentencing.

THE CHAPEL FOR EVERYMAN ❺

De Allemanskapel van Sint Joris
Oudezijds Achterburgwal 100, 1012DS Amsterdam
• Tel.: 020 626 66 34 • Services at 8:45am and 7:30pm every day
except Sunday
• Torah reading every Friday evening

A place
of prayer
where everyone
is welcome

Far from recollections of the Alteration (see below), the Chapel for Everyman is a surprising place where believers of all the Christian and Jewish faiths are welcome. Accordingly, the church presents symbols of several religions: an "ambom"- a typical protestant lectern, where the bible stands; a catholic altar; an orthodox Iconostasis - a movable screen (symbolizing the division between earth and heaven) which can be used to separate the choir from the rest of the church; and, at the entrance to the chapel, a baptismal font or Jordan, typical of the evangelistic tradition. The floor motifs, in concentric circles, are intended to represent the impulses that the Creator gives to our world, as well as the different circles of involvement of members of the community. Finally, the chandelier, in the form of a terrestrial globe, symbolizes our devotion. Always in the true spirit of the place, the services are led by a selected priest, pastor or rabbi.

THE ALTERATION: FROM CATHOLIC TO PROTESTANT

On 26 May 1578, the administration of the town of Amsterdam passed from the hands of the Catholics, who had ultimately joined the revolt against the Spaniards, into the hands of a Protestant Orange council. This is a key stage in the town's history, called "Alteratie" or the Alteration.

The churches and chapels were confiscated and became Protestant or were used for secular activities. The Catholics found themselves forbidden to practice their religion in public.

Although they were not persecuted, until 1798 they had to find secret places to gather, like the well-known Church of the Good Lord in the Attic (Amstelkring).

THE CONVENTS OF AMSTERDAM

In the Middle Ages, Amsterdam had more than 20 convents. Most of them were run by nuns and were situated outside the town ramparts, in the southwest part of the town, between the Rokin, the Nes and the Kloveniersburgwal. Today only the street names recall this rich religious life. The most notable are Bethaniënstraat, for the convent of Saint Mary Magdalen of Bethany, Monnikenstraat, from the name of the Franciscan monastery, or Reguliersstraat, from the name of the Regular sisters.

Another amusing name of a little street is "Gebed zonder end", meaning "endless prayer"; in this street there were so many monasteries that one could always hear praying.

HERBALISTS' SHOP JACOB HOOY & CO   ❻

Kloveniersburgwal 12, 1012CT Amsterdam
• Tel.: 072 505 27 44
• Open Tuesday to Friday 10am to 6pm, Monday 1pm to 6pm,
Saturday 10am to 5pm, Thursday night open till 9pm

> **When "opium" and "tobacco" were considered remedies...**

Jacob Hooy, the herbalist, was the son of a sailor and when only 21 years old, he opened in 1743 his shop, Jacob Hooy & Co, housed in a pretty 16th century building near the Nieuwmarkt square. In those day, the plants and spices, brought back from the Asia by the ships of the United East India Company, (known as the V.O.C.) were traded on this market square and hence it was practical for him to open his retail business nearby.

Today the shop still retains its original décor, composed of rows of drawers and shelves holding medicinal herbs, teas and spices.

The small barrels on the shelves were especially made to measure for the shop, and are reminiscent of their larger 'brothers' which were used to protect these products during their transport in the holds of the V.O.C.'s ships. They are labelled with the Latin names of the medicinal plants they contain. It is interesting to note that, in those days, both tobacco and opium were considered to be remedies for illness.

Before the shop was enlarged, the counter at the rear of the shop, was located to the right of the shop's entrance and the bar, hanging from the ceiling was used to hold reels of paper for packing the herbs and preparations. Note also the beautiful scales. The one decorated with two entwined serpents, came from the Netherlands Indies, whilst its more classic companion dates from 1706. The sales area at the rear of the shop, used to house the office.

Finally, it is difficult to know if the external shutters are the original ones. Were they for protecting the shop against possible theft, at a time when spices were valued more precious than gold.

Today, the shop no longer belongs to Jacob Hooy's descendants, but it still maintains its specialized expertise and knowledge of plants, flowers, fruits, roots and seeds, and, more than 200 years later, is able to offer, a range of over 1500 natural and original products.

PLANT MARKET In the 17th Century, plants were traded on the Nieuwmarkt square, both those grown locally and also from Rijnsburg and Hillegom. Today, Rijnsburg, near Leiden, is the location of one of the largest flower auctions in the Netherlands.

THE SYMMETRICAL HOUSE
OF THE TRIP BROTHERS

Kloveniersburgwal 29, 1011 JV Amsterdam

> *Two brothers, two identical houses*

The Trip house was built between 1660 and 1664 for the brothers Louis and Hendrik Trip, who inherited their Uncle Louys de Geer's business in Sweden, consisting of large iron and copper mines, foundries, forges and arms factories. When their business prospered, they decided to build a large mansion in Amsterdam, to provide both of them with accommodation and enable them to continue their activities together. Standing on the opposite side of the canal, around No 26 of the Kloveniersburgwal, one can admire the perfect symmetry of the building, which hides two adjoining houses. They are separated by an impressive wall, half a metre thick, aligned with the central windows, which were originally closed. It's interesting to know that although not apparent from the exterior, the symmetry extends even to the interior arrangement of the mansion's rooms. The mansion was built by Justus Vingboons, brother of the more famous architect, Philips Vingboons. The Trip brothers probably made his acquaintance in Sweden, where he worked between 1653 and 1656. They asked him to design a house worthy of their status, one of city's richest and most influential regent families. Apart from the mansion's dimensions, a 22m. wide gable, the largest of any private residence in Amsterdam, the Corinthian style columns, give a majestic character to the building. Notable are also the chimneys in the form of mortars, together with the decor of canons and olive branches, a reference to its owner's being arms dealers. In the interior, the finesse of the delicately painted vaulted ceilings indicates the proprietors' desire to display their affluence. The Trip brothers' descendants continued to live in the mansion until 1814, when it became home to Louis Bonaparte's Royal Academy of Arts, Letters and Sciences, founded in 1808. The Academy's collections remained on display in the Trippenhuis until they received a new home, the Rijksmuseum in 1885.

TO SEE NEARBY

THE LITTLE TRIP HOUSE
Kloveniersburgwal 26, 1012CV Amsterdam

The story goes that when the Trip house at 29 Kloveniersburgwal was finished, the coachman sighed and remarked that if only he had a house as big as the front door he would be the happiest of men. The Trip brothers took him at his word and, with the left over materials from their house, had a little Trip house built for him opposite the big one.

In 1639, Rembrandt painted a portrait of Maria Trip, their cousin, in which she is shown wearing a fine dress of lace embroidered with gold. This portrait, now famous, can be seen in the Rijksmuseum.

KOESTRAAT: THE STREET OF THE COW

After the Alteration of 1578, the Amsterdam council bought the majority of the land occupied by the convent of Bethany (see opposite page). The Street of the Cow has retained its name as a memory of the meadows where the sisters pastured their herd.

Jan van der Heyden, the Dutch Leonardo da Vinci, lived at No 5 for 30 years. Behind his house was a small factory, a sort of inventor's workshop. One of his most notable inventions was that of the street-light, around 1670. In 1690, he announced the invention of the fire-hose. The Tsar of Russia, Peter the Great, could not persuade him to accompany him to Russia, but bought a great quantity of these fire-hoses for a price of 385 florins each. Later, van der Heyden became famous as a landscape painter. In 1868, a school was built on the site of his house, and in 1912 a plaque was installed to commemorate the former presence of this famous inhabitant (1632-1712).

At **numbers 7-9-11**, pretty façades with "neck gables" are decorated with illustrations representing the Virtues. At No 7 a woman carries a bible for Faith, at No 9 a mother with her child represents Love, and at No 11 a woman with an anchor symbolizes Hope.

At numbers 10-12, a door constructed in 1633 by the architect Pieter de Keyzer (son of Hendrick) is decorated with a high-relief depicting Bacchus, surrounded by vine leaves. This door gave access, earlier on, to **the Guild of Wine Merchants**.

Jan Pietersz. Sweelinck (1562-1621) lived at No 15 at the end of the 16th century. One of the most celebrated Dutch organists, Sweelinck, became organist of the Oude Kerk Church at the age of 15 and played there for 44 years. His work inspired German organists who regarded him as a master of their art.

THE CONCERTS OF THE CONVENT OF BETHANY

9

Bethaniën klooster, Barndesteeg 6B, 1012BV Amsterdam
• Tel.: 020 625 00 78 • Admission free concert by the students of
the Music School every Friday at 12:30pm, except during school holidays

The Convent of Mary Magdalen of Bethany was originally a convent for
women who wanted to do penance after a dissolute life. In 1492, the chapter
of the parent establishment, at The Hague, gave the convent the right to
build its own chapel with its own curate and its own cemetery. The Convent
of Bethany also bred cattle and brewed beer. It was closed in 1578. Only
the North wing along the Barndesteeg, restored in 1980, was preserved.

The remains of the old convent building feature a 15th century vaulted
crypt, above which is a hall two stories high, and a loft which provides living
quarters for young musicians.

Nowadays, beneath the centuries-old oak ceiling of the Convent of Bethany
a small music centre is situated. It can seat 120 people, and with its thick
walls, has an excellent acoustic. On Friday afternoons the Convent offers
young students of music the possibility to familiarize themselves with
performing in public.

THE PROVERBS OF THE FIRST SAINT NICHOLAS CHURCH

⑩

Oude Kerk, Oudekerksplein 23, 1012GX Amsterdam
• Tel.: 020 625 82 84
• Open Monday to Saturday from 11am to 5pm, Sunday 1pm to 5pm
• Entry charge

> *When money doesn't come out of my behind...*

Originally built in the form of a three-hall church around 1300, the church of Saint Nicholas was constantly enlarged. The side aisles were lengthened and chapels added in proportion to the town's growth until, nearly 3 centuries later, it had become an imposing Gothic Renaissance-style basilica.

In 1566, the revolt of the iconoclasts (Beeldenstorm), a popular movement decrying the worship of statues in churches, took place. Here, too, statues were removed, even though an image on the ceiling, at the crossing of the nave and the transept, still bears witness to its former patron: Saint Nicholas. Taken over by the Protestants in 1578, Saint Nicholas church acquired its current name - Oude Kerk (the Old Church). A phrase alluding to this period can be seen on the grille to the choir entrance: "'t misbruyk in God weer-afgedaen in 't jaer zeventichacht (XV)" (the misuse of God once again removed in the year 78 of the 1500s).

The choir possesses superb, and rare, stalls, which illustrate Dutch proverbs in a remarkable way. The clothing styles of the people carved on the miseri-cords follow the fashion of the 1480's, leading one to suppose that this was the period when these stalls were carved.

It is amusing to try to determine the proverbs illustrated by these scenes. The scene of one man attacking and another trying to calm him, for instance, represents the cardinal sin of anger and the virtue of temperance. A few rows down one finds an illustration of the damaging effects of alcohol and of other proverbs such as "money has no value in the face of death."

On the opposite side, proverbs like "one should sail when the wind blows" (meaning one should "catch the ball on the bounce"), "money doesn't come out of my behind" (or "money doesn't grow on trees"), and "stuck between a rock and a hard place" are illustrated. Finally, the proverb "he who wants to open his mouth like an oven must open wide" reminds us not to lose ourselves in vain efforts.

Saskia van Uylenburg, Rembrandt's wife, was buried in Oude Kerk in 1642.
Each year, when the weather is sunny, on 9 March at 8:39am, a ray of light, the first sunbeam of spring, lights up her tomb.

In 1978, during the restoration of the Church, an artist painted his self-portrait in the faux marble under the organ.

TO SEE NEARBY

FEMININE BUST IN BRONZE ⑪
Oudekerksplein, 1012GX Amsterdam

Slightly to the right when exiting the Oude Kerk church, amongst the cobblestones, one can notice an interesting feminine bust in bronze. One breast seems to be cupped by what may be a man's hand. In this work of art from 1993, the artist must have been inspired by the bodies on display in the windows of the neighbouring streets.

HOMAGE TO PROSTITUTES ⑫
Oudekerksplein, 1012GX Amsterdam opposite No 42

On this open space in front of the Oude Kerk's tower entrance, a bronze statue representing a prostitute in a proud pose was installed in March and is called "Belle". She stands with a slightly arrogant air, looking down on passers-by. The statue was sculpted by Els Rijerse at the initiative of Mariska Majoor, an ex-prostitute. Its aim is to incite respect for the millions of women and men in the world who make their living in this secular business.

THE TEA AND COFFEE MUSEUM ⑬

Geels & Co, Warmoesstraat 67, 1012HX Amsterdam
• Tel.: 020 624 06 83
• Open Saturday 2pm till 4:30pm and by appointment. Free entrance

Dating from the 19th century, the very attractive shop Geels & Co contains an entertaining collection of machines and utensils used for preparing tea and coffee, from the raw materials to the table.

A 19th century witness to an 18th century epic

In 1863, Antonius Geels opened his business in colonial products, which at the time was called "tea, coffee and confectionery". In 1866, he transferred the shop to No 67 Warmoesstraat, in a building called the Golden Head, "Het Gulden Hooft", which dates from 1567 but whose simple cornice façade in Louis XV style dates from 1686. Wholesaler to boutiques, herbalist shops and grocers until the First World War, Geels & Co then began to sell retail, and more recently on the Internet.

Few things have changed in this attractive shop, still run today by Esther Geels, a descendant of Antonius, and where one can still absorb the 19th century ambiance.

An old wooden staircase leads up to the first floor. There you can find the machines used to sort coffee beans by size, to roast them and to grind them. Note the roasting machine in the centre, which has an ingenious mechanism that allows a significant quantity of beans to be put to roast on a wood stove. More than 100 coffee mills are on display.

COFFEE, FROM ETHIOPIA TO AMSTERDAM AND TO BRAZIL

The United East India Company (V.O.C., see page 50) enabled the Dutch, among others, to discover new botanical species, including the first coffee plant from Ethiopia, which was kept in the Botanical Garden ("Hortus botanicus") (see page 193). Brought back from the town of Kaffa in Ethiopia (hence the name coffee) in the course of the expedition of 1706, it was conserved and adapted by the botanist Caspar Commelin in Amsterdam. When King Louis XIV visited Amsterdam, he was offered a coffee plant, which later found its way to Brazil on a French ship. In the Golden Age, Amsterdam was the leading port in Europe for the import of tea and coffee. The tea exchange used to be in Nes street, where the Frascati theatre is now located. It was later moved into the Zorcher Exchange, and then into the Berlage Exchange.

THE GABLE STONE FROM RIGA ⓮

Oudezijds Voorburgwal 14, 1012GD Amsterdam

> *The arms
> of Riga, traces
> of commerce with
> the Baltics*

The gable stone, with its crossed keys, represents the arms of the town of Riga, capital of present day Lithuania, on the Baltic Sea.

This plaque can be found on the lovely step-gabled house constructed around 1650 by Wessel Becker, a Riga merchant. The house is very typical of its time and is built on an inner wooden structure that supports the brick walls. On the cross wall, one can see that the upper part of the house juts out: it rests on a horizontal timber beam.

In 1356, the commercial towns of Zutphen, Deventer, Kampen, Zwolle and Tiel grouped together to form a commercial alliance, called "De Hanze" (The Hanseatic League). Associated with towns in Germany, Belgium and as far as the Baltic States, they set up a trade route. Goods were transported by sea and by river on cogs, shallow broad boats from 15 to 30 metres long. Trading extended as far as England or Spain. The goods traded included salt, grains, fish, wood, wine, beer, animal skins, cloth and wool. Later, the organization specialized in trading luxury goods.

In 1438, another commercial organization, known as "Moeder Negotie" or "Mother Commerce", developed on the Baltic Sea, a top location for Dutch trade. It was given this name because it was so lucrative.

Almost 3000 movements of Dutch boats to the Baltic region and Sweden can be traced in the 16th century. The Swedish Royal Family and Swedish notables spoke fluent Dutch, proof of the supremacy of Dutch merchants in this part of the world.

SAINT OLOF'S CHAPEL ⑮

To see from the exterior on the Zeedijk, 1012AN Amsterdam
• Entry via the Hotel Barbizon, Prins Hendrikkade, 59-72, 1012AD Amsterdam
• Visit on request by phoning: 020 556 45 64

The oldest chapel in Amsterdam can be visited by appointment

S aint Olof's chapel is the oldest in Amsterdam. Built on the Zeedijk around 1450, it was placed under the protection of Saint Odolphus of Brabant, patron Saint of dikes. At the end of the 15th century, the chapel was enlarged and the extension was named the Jerusalem Chapel as, in the 15th and 16th centuries, it was the meeting place of the "Fathers of Jerusalem," or pilgrims who had made the voyage to the Holy Land. The chapel is in Gothic style, but the doorways, one on the Zeedijk dating from 1644 and two on the Nieuwebrugsteeg dating from 1620 and 1671, are in the Dutch Renaissance style. Look for the renovated high-relief on the Zeedijk entry. It represents a supine skeleton with the caption "spes altera vitae" (in the hope of another life). After the Alteration of 1578, the municipality confiscated the chapel and used it as a commercial exchange before giving it to the Reformed Church in 1602. At that time it was called the "Oudezijds Kapel". The last mass was celebrated in 1912. The church was subsequently used for various purposes, including, notably, the weekly cheese market in the 1950s. St. Olof's chapel was closed in 1964 because it threatened to collapse. A renovation project wasn't proposed until 1991. The city, along with the Association for Historic Monuments and the Barbizon Hotel, undertook a complete restoration. The church is now used as a conference hall and is linked to the Barbizon Hotel by an underground passage.

SPES ALTERA VITÆ

SINT-OLOFSPOORT The Saint Olof's gate included two large stone towers on the town side plus a bridge over the canal and an outer fortification. They were part of the surrounding wall of Amsterdam and were built in 1370 along with the lengthening of the main street of the town, called Kerkstraat, which is today known as Warmoesstraat. The gate was used till 1425 and was put down in 1618. The passage between the Warmoestraat and the Zeedijk remains known as Saint Olof's gate.

AN ULTRA-MODERN CAR PARK
The Barbizon Hotel has an underground park for 25 cars. Its entrance is operated electronically. You park by driving onto a platform, which is then activated by the porter from his control panel and moved automatically to an underground space.

ONE OF THE LAST TIMBER-FRAMED HOUSES ⑯
IN AMSTERDAM

Zeedijk 1, 1012AN Amsterdam
• Tel.: 020 626 84 01
• Open Sunday to Thursday 3pm to 1am
and Friday to Saturday 3pm to 3am

> *Looks like someone stayed at the monkey's*

Built in 1550, the house at No 1 Zeedijk is one of the only remaining fully timber-framed houses in Amsterdam. The wooden construction rests on brick walls but the entire timber frame is original.

The building was constructed "op de vlucht", meaning that it leans forward a little. Each floor was built to jut out more than 25 cm beyond the one below, so that rainwater would fall from each level straight down to the street, and to facilitate hauling goods up to the upper floors or to the loft.

This building has been an inn ever since it was built. Located near the sea, it welcomed many sailors who brought back monkeys from their voyages to distant lands. They would offer these animals to the landlord, either as gifts or to pay their debts.

The landlord liked to keep them in cages, even though they always attracted parasites. When somebody in the neighbourhood scratched, passers-by would remark "to be sure he's been staying at the monkey house". This remark became a common expression to refer to someone who has worries.

The ground floor is occupied by the café called In 't Aepjen (Aepjen is the old Dutch spelling for monkey), while the upper floors house bedrooms belonging to the Barbizon Hotel.

Another timber-framed house to see in Amsterdam is at No 34 Begijnhof (entrance on het Spui Square).
Wood was used in several other houses in Amsterdam but, except for the two mentioned here, only their wooden frames date from the 16th century.

While, in the Middle Ages, houses were mainly built from timber, the great fires of 1421 and 1452 caused the prohibition of this highly inflammable material, at least for the load-bearing walls, which also made it possible to build higher houses. Wood being a light material, it required smaller foundations than for brick houses.
For lack of natural sources of stone, most houses were built of bricks. The rare stones used in construction were called "Bentheim" from the name of the quarries in Germany, near the frontier, where they were extracted.

TO SEE NEARBY

GABLE STONE OF "THE VIEW OF THE DUNES" ⑰

At number 82 Zeedijk is a house with an original gable stone inscribed "Duinzicht" or "View of the Dunes", which evidently records the past (see below). When walking along the street, or the former dike, one is aware of its height as the city spreads out below on the even-numbered side of the street.

THE HISTORY OF THE ZEEDIJK

The "Zeedijk" or "sea dike" was a dike that protected Amsterdam from the Zuiderzee. Formerly a sea, today the Zuiderzee is no more than a lake and has been called IJsselmeer since the construction of the great dike, the "Afsluitdijk", in 1932.

What would Amsterda m be without its dikes ? It would be, no doubt, marshes and peat-filled swamps, like Connemara in Ireland. It would be uninhabitable, it seems, and yet there are traces of human presence from 300 BC onward at Weesp, 12km east of Amsterdam. Embankments built from river sand had already made it possible to dry out the land.

The first dikes were only constructed starting in 1000 AD. One can find the names of the villages of Sloten, Osdorp and Schellingwoude in the tax registers of Floris V of Holland dating from the 13th century. Later, around 1500, lakes were pumped dry, thanks to the power of windmills, which led eventually to the creation of polders.

In the 12th century a great dike was constructed, stretching from the Gooi region as far as the dunes of Kennermerland (in the region of Haarlem), to protect against flooding from the Zuiderzee.

On this dike was a road suitable for vehicles, creating the first element of the road network in Amsterdam. The Zeedijk (or Saint Anthony's Dike) was part of this great feat of construction, like the Haarlemmerdijk.

THE HISTORY OF THE CHINESE IN AMSTERDAM

About 10,000 Chinese live in Amsterdam, of whom 80% work in the restaurant business.

The presence of the Dutch in China is much older than that of the Chinese in Holland, since Taiwan came under Dutch control in 1624. The immigration of the Chinese to Amsterdam developed at the same time as the intensification of trade with the Orient.

The Chinese were recruited as cheap labour for merchant shipping, as sailors or cooks. After the great strike of 1911 of the Dutch sailor men, the recruitment of Chinese labour grew strongly and the number of Chinese registered as Amsterdam residents leaped from around 100 to more than 2000 after 1915.

Once they landed in Rotterdam or Amsterdam, Chinese immigrants were taken in charge by their local network and housed in dormitories near the harbour, the forerunner of what became China-Town. They were followed by Chinese merchants who set up business in the Nieuwmarkt district. In addition to the trade of Asian goods, they set up small guesthouses, laundries and restaurants.

Up until the Second World War, the Chinese population in Holland scarcely exceeded a few thousand, the large majority of which were men. It was in the second half of the 20th century that Chinese immigration really took off.

In the late 1940s, at the end of the Dutch colonial era in Indonesia, numerous Indonesian Chinese preferred to flee to The Netherlands, where they integrated easily, thanks to their level of education and their knowledge of the language.

Other Chinese emigrated from Southern China to escape the Communist takeover.

Lastly, Hong Kong Chinese used their status as British subjects to emmigrate to Holland.

The highlight of the neighbourhood is clearly the famous Lotus Flower Buddhist Temple (Fo Guang Shan He Hua, Nos 106-118 Zeedijk).

Note also the bilingual street signs in this quarter - in Mandarin and Dutch.

On nearby Geldersekade, a clinic receives and treats people using traditional Chinese medicine, including acupuncture (Chinese Medical Centre Nos 67-73 Geldersekade).

Various Chinese herbal remedies, concocted on demand, can be bought here.

TO SEE NEARBY

THE SUGAR LOAVES ABOVE THE IN DE OLOFSPOORT PUBLIC HOUSE ⓲

Proeflokaal In de Olofspoort, Nieuwebrugsteeg 13, 1012AG Amsterdam
• Tel.: 020 624 39 18 • Open Wednesday and Thursday 4 pm to 00:30 am,
Fridays and Saturdays 4 pm to 1:30 am and Sunday 3 pm to 10 pm

De Olofspoort is a public house located in a building dating from 1619.
Built by the architect Hendrick de Keyser on the site of the former Saint Olof
gate (see page 4) - hence the name Olofspoort - it has a lovely stepped gable
that is a fine example of Dutch Renaissance style. The colorful gable stone
plaque is an interesting testimony to the history of this house. Three men in
17th century costumes are depicted, probable proof that the house was built
around that time. At first it housed a sugar refinery, as the stone's inscription
"in de lompen" indicates, lomp being the word for the sugar loaves in those
days. Later, the building housed a bakery. It wasn't converted into a public
house until 1986. While appreciating the interior renovated in 17th century
style, one can sample over 60 different Dutch and Belgian genevers. The text
"Hoede Kramer" was discovered during the recent renovation of the gable
stone. A hat seller, Jan Reinerts Coster, was the first owner of this house.
The step gable was created in the style of Lieven de Key, a Flemish architect
who introduced the Renaissance style to Haarlem at the beginning of
the 17th century. This gable has numerous steps decorated with tiny
white blocks and a pilaster.

THE STORY OF THE "POT HOUSES"

Mind the small shelter in front of this house: it is a "pothuis". In the
Middle Ages, the houses had a well on the street side, embedded in
a little wooden house, to make it accessible from the cellar. Hence,
the name "puthuis", meaning house of the well.
During the 17th century, when the houses were rebuilt in bricks,
most of the pothuizen disappeared. Some remained and were
mostly used as scullery to store kitchen utensils.
They were sometimes used by craftsmen like shoemakers or even
as housing. In 1820, building pothuizen was forbidden. Luckily,
many of them remained.

THE "IN COIGNAC" GABLE STONE ⑲

Geldersekade 97, 1011EM Amsterdam

From wine to brandy then to cognac

The house at No 97 Geldersekade was built at the very beginning of 17th century by wine merchant Willem Hendrickszoon. Between the 1st and 2nd floors, a lovely stone carving shows a town, and is inscribed "in Coignac".

In the course of restoring this stone in 1993, research indicated that it was indeed a representation of the French town Cognac, in the Charente region, whose links with Amsterdam were significant (see below).

Behind the crenellated town walls, semi-circular bastions, town gates, bridges and houses with towers, churches and chapels are clearly depicted. To the left of the scene, one can see a large castle and even people walking alongside the river as well as a rider on horseback, maybe the Knight de la Croix Marron.

THE TOWN OF AMSTERDAM AT THE ORIGIN OF THE INVENTION OF COGNAC...

Cognac owes much to The Netherlands. In the 16th century, the town of Cognac carried on a thriving trade from its salt warehouses. Dutch boats, which transported wheat grain from eastern Europe to western France, loaded salt for their return journey, and later wine, with the growth of Poitou's wine production. This wine rapidly became popular but didn't travel well owing to its low alcohol content. In the 17th century, an Amsterdam apothecary discovered that, by heating it, then adding water, an interesting flavour and better conservation could be achieved. This wine was called Brandwijn or "burned wine", whence the name Brandy.

The Knight de la Croix Marron, who came from the Charente region, thought of distilling this mix a second time, allowing the alcohol to transform into permanent eau de vie, thus giving birth to a new drink: Cognac.

THE SHIP-CHANDLER'S WAREHOUSE

Ship-chandler's warehouse • Geldersekade 8, 1012BH Amsterdam
• Visit by appointment by phoning 06 46 388 567

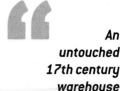

An untouched 17th century warehouse

By appointment, one can visit the remarkable historic Ship-chandler's Warehouse, a 17th century store whose interior fixtures and fittings have remained almost intact. The counter, the scales, the beer casks and ranges of drawers have all been preserved. In the Golden Age, the warehouse was at the service of ships' captains who came there to stock up their ships before leaving for the high seas. The shop itself was on the lower level, the upper floors being used for storing merchandise. Here, one sampled and ordered goods, particularly food, which was then transferred by small boats to the ships; at that time the harbour was fairly close by. A still-visible relic from the past is the ladder on the quay in front of the building, where boats came alongside. The building was constructed in 1624, as confirmed by the inscription on a stone in the cellar. The style of the rear façade on Oudezijds Kolk (1 A-D), with its pointed gable, should not deceive - it was radically renovated in the 18th century. Notable is the festooned ornamentation of the horizontal cornice in Louis XVI style dating from around 1775.

Also notable is the very interesting tympanum or decorated arched recess over the door. It represents a barrel of tobacco and two plaited reed baskets filled with tobacco leaves, indicating that the original business here was tobacco. Also to be seen inside, on the wall above the staircase, is a wooden sculpture of Jean Niko, from whose name the word nicotine is derived. It was clearly around 1800 that the shop's purpose changed. The building is a typical example of a merchant's store. The 3 middle windows, which were most certainly closed by shutters in the past, gave access to the loft, where goods were stocked after having been hauled up by the use of the hoisting beam. The owners entirely restored the building 25 years ago, while preserving the period details.

The reception hall on the 1st floor, decorated in the 17th century style, can be rented to hold dinners for groups of twenty to fifty people. Cocktails can be served in the billiard room, which has been beautifully preserved.

BRIEF HISTORY OF THE V.O.C.-THE FIRST LIMITED COMPANY

The creation of the Verenigde Oost-Indische Company or V.O.C. (United East India Company) in 1602 contributed greatly to the historic power of The Netherlands. Indeed, at the height of its influence, the Dutch Republic controlled the second richest trading post network in the world, after the Portuguese.

The East Indies venture was a costly and very risky enterprise, but also an extremely profitable one. The rich traders of the United Provinces were well aware of this, which is why they joined forces to create, by the charter of 20 March1602, the first limited company in the world financed by shares, with sole trading rights in the East, from South Africa to Japan.

The permanent character of the capital - linked to a fund-raising levy for each expedition -, the number of shareholders, as well as the scale of the capital, ensured that the V.O.C. had exemplary financial stability. In addition, the V.O.C. was endowed with a range of regal powers in Asia by the "Staten generaal": it could found colonies, raise its own army, declare war and sign treaties, exercise justice, mint coinage and raise taxes.

The V.O.C. was a decentralized organization, based on 6 independent regional chambers, each representing a town and its surroundings (Amsterdam, Middelburg (Zeeland), Delft, Rotterdam, Hoorn and Enkhuizen). Each chamber elected its representatives, who formed the general direction or Heren Zeventien. Owned by its shareholders, the V.O.C. had but one aim: profit.

It was the first structured organization of a merchant middle class which threw off feudal privileges, in short the first manifestation of capitalism. The V.O.C.'s trade was notable for spices, particularly pepper, nutmeg, cinnamon and cloves, and also porcelain and silk. But the ships' cargoes included tobacco, rice, tea, coffee and sugar, as well as iron, tin and steel, and certainly opium.

The company also enriched itself through regional commerce carried on from Batavia, throughout the whole of Asia and as far as China and Japan. In the face of Catholic conversion attempts by the Portuguese, Japan closed its ports in 1639 to all ships except those of the Dutch, who kept a trading post on Deshima Island, near Nagasaki, until 1859.

Over nearly two centuries, the V.O.C. sent almost a million people to Asia aboard 4721 ships, of which 3356 returned, with roughly 2.5 million tons of merchandise.

The V.O.C. was slightly preceded by the British East India Company founded in 1600, but, as the first to issue shares, it served as the model for numerous other companies: the French India Co, founded in 1664 by Colbert, the Danish Asiatik Kompagnie founded in 1670, and the Swedish Ostindiska Kompaniet founded in 1731.

THE DECORATED PLAQUE OF THE WEEPING WOMEN OF THE V.O.C. ㉑

Prins Hendrikkade 94-95, 1012AE Amsterdam
• Tel.: 020 428 82 91
• Café open daily 11am till 1pm, Monday till 8pm.
• Saturday and Sunday till 3am

> **The farewells of the wives left behind by the mariners who sailed away on the V.O.C's ships**

The V.O.C café is housed in the Schreierstoren, one of the towers of the town ramparts in the Middle Ages. Constructed in 1480, the tower originally provided direct access to the sea. As the ground level has since been raised, a part of the tower is now below ground level.

The tower bears a remarkable plaque that dates from 1569 and represents a weeping woman. Beside it is an inscription, "Scrayer-Houvk", meaning literally "the corner of the weeping women". This was indeed the place of farewells for the women-folk of mariners who set off to distant lands on the ships of the V.O.C. (see double-page following) and whose safe return home was uncertain.

Some people maintain, however, that the name Schreierstoren derives, instead, from the Dutch for "leaning", which would be an allusion to the aspect of the tower rather than to weeping women.

There is also a commemorative plaque that was mounted in 1946 to celebrate the 350th anniversary of the departure of the first convoy of 4 V.O.C. ships led by Cornelis Houtman. The ships departed from this same spot, heading for the East Indies. Only three ships returned in 1597. The bird symbolizes the one that was lost.

Another plaque, in bronze, was affixed by the Greenwich Village Historical Society to commemorate the departure, on 4 April 1609, of Henry Hudson for America, on board the ship "De halve Maen" (The half moon) armed by the V.O.C. He gave his name to the Hudson River.

THE GABLE STONES OF THE V.O.C.

Apart from the plaque on the tower of the weeping women, numerous other carved stone plaques illustrating the oriental adventures of the Dutch are to be found in Amsterdam. The following are some of the most interesting.

On the **Oudezijds Voorburgwal**, at No 14 on the side of the house, a small plaque represents three rather jovial sailors in single file. This plaque was originally on No 20 Bethaniëndwarsstraat, alongside the East India House, where the sailors received their pay. This small plaque was no doubt used to publicize one of the numerous inns in this area at the time.

Also on the **Oudezijds Voorburgwal** at No 136, is a fine ornamental façade in carved wood, representing Admiral Cornelis Tromp.

He is presented as a hero in a typically 17th century setting.

His rank of Admiral can be recognized from several details: his breastplate, the globe and a nautical chart, but also his staff and a medal. On the right of the globe a cannon can also be seen. Admiral Tromp distinguished himself by his victory against the English in 1652.

Near the **Oudezijdskolk**, several decorative plaques have been assembled on a small wall. These plaques were saved from old houses that were to be demolished.

The stone representing a recumbent lioness "de liggende leeuwin" came from No 14 Kleine Kattenburgerstraat and was fixed here in 1960. The prominent nipples and lack of a mane show clearly that it is a lioness. In the background one can see a cape, a point of land materialized by wooden buoys that were placed along the coast as markers to aid navigation.

In March 1622, a V.O.C. ship called "the lioness" ("leeuwin") reached the most westerly point of Australia, which has since then been called Cape Leeuwin.

On **Nieuwe Uilenburgerstraat**, at No 114, an inscription confirms that the content of the large sack depicted is coffee; note to the left and the right respectively a flower and a fruit of the coffee plant.

On the exterior wall of the **Amsterdam Museum** is a magnificent plaque, which was originally at Warmoesstraat No 174, and that represents a merchant negotiating a cotton deal. On the cotton bales are written details of their quality and their transport itinerary.

On the **Tweede Rozendwarsstraat**, at No 21, is a plaque representing a sailor in full dress uniform. This gable stone undoubtedly marked the house of an officer of the V.O.C.

On **Tichelstraat** at No 33, at the top of the lovely "neck" gable, the inscription "Batavia 1737" encircles a sword and a laurel wreath on the background of an orange shield - the emblem of the first Dutch trading post in Indonesia, Batavia.

Initially it comprised only a fort with four towers, named after the 4 Dutch provinces: Gelderland, Zeeland, Holland and West Friesland.

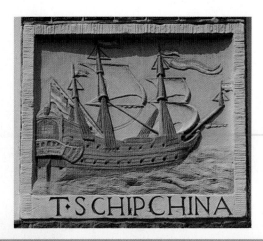

The V.O.C. installed their head office there. As the town grew, it changed its name to Djakarta.

On the **Buiten Brouwersstraat**, at No 20, is a lovely decorative plaque recently renovated in four colours. It recalls the 3-masted ship the "China", constructed in 1676 for the Amsterdam Chamber of the V.O.C., at the V.O.C. shipyards on the Isle of Oostenburg, to make return voyages to the East. This fine ship fulfilled its purpose by making 5 return voyages to the Batavia trading post between 1677 and 1691, each journey taking from 6 to 9 months.

Three coffee pots illustrate the decorative plaque at No 38 **St Nicolaasstraat**. They symbolize the three trading posts on the East African coast – Mocha (on the Red Sea in Yemen), Basra (in Irak) and Gamron (today the harbour Bandar Abbas in Iran) – from which coffee was imported. This plaque is attributed to the establishment of a coffee shop at this location in 1742.

THE HOUSE OF THE SHIPOWNERS

Scheepvaarthuis, Grand Hotel and café-restaurant Amrâth Amsterdam
Prins Hendrikkade 108-114, 1011AP Amsterdam
• Guided tour each Sunday at 10:30am by reservation
• Tel.: 020 552 00 00

*One of
the very first
productions of the
Amsterdam School*

The surprising House of the Shipowners (Scheepvaarthuis), was built in the early 20th century by architect Johan van der Mey, with the assistance of his friends Michel de Klerk and Pieter Kramer. It was the first production of these co-founders of the style known as the Amsterdam School (see page 270). The Van Gendt brothers undertook the construction of the concrete skeleton and the stained glass was the work of glassmaker Willem Bogtman. The Scheepvaarthuis was conceived as an office building. From the time of its construction between 1913 and 1916, an extension was planned. It was built 12 years later, providing space for 6 ship owners. The last company left the building in 1981. The building, triangular in shape, was built from a concrete skeleton into which bricks of 200 different shapes and sizes were inserted. Notable is the remarkable harmony between the workmanship of the façade and the decor of the interior: both exhibit the same attention to symbols. The exterior, on the corner of Prins Hendrikkade and Binnenkant, is reminiscent of the prow of a ship. At the entrance are four sculptures by H. van den Eijnde representing the four oceans and, at roof level, there are lovely statues of Neptune and Hermes, gods of the sea and of travel. High up on the sides of the building are 29 statues by Hildo Krop representing famous Dutchmen of the maritime world; their birth dates are engraved below them. The cornice ornaments portray maritime scenes. Built on the same spot from which the first expedition to the East Indies set off in 1596, led by Cornelis Houtman, the building possesses, around the entrance, illustrations, images and symbols recalling the wealth of maritime activity in The Netherlands. As you stand in the entrance before the rotating doors, look up to admire Ursa Major and the north star recreated by the lanterns on the ceiling. Do not miss the superb stained-glass dome depicting the constellations on the 3rd floor, or the grand conference room decorated with exotic hardwood.

TO SEE NEARBY

BANTAMMERBRUG
From Geldersekade to Bantammerstraat, 1011 Amsterdam

Built in 1914 by van der Mey, the Bantammerbrug bridge was very poorly received by the inhabitants of the neighbourhood where it was built. Its School Amsterdam style was very avant-garde at the time. It was named the Bantammerbrug in honour of the town on the Isle of Java from which Cornelis Houtman brought back his first cargoes of spices in 1597.

THE STRONG ROOM
OF THE 'BERLAGE' STOCK EXCHANGE

Damrak 277, 1012 ZJ Amsterdam
• Guided visit by reservation with the Artifex
organization • Tel.: 020 620 81 12

A strong room from the turn of the century

A remarkable safe-filled vault is located in the basement of the former Commodity Exchange, designed by Berlage, under the café that now occupies the former main entrance and entrance hall.

The safes were constructed in 1902 by the Lips Co of Dordrecht, lock specialists from 1871 to 1998, and whose name is still associated with this skill today. The name, painted in Art Deco style script, is to be found on the interior of the doors of the individual safes. They were available for rent by individuals wishing to safeguard their papers and valuables.

The strong room is secured by an extremely thick door that weighs two tonnes. Notably fine are the brass closing mechanisms and the lovely gold decoration.

The whole premises were renovated in 2001 and one can see them either during a guided visit or during one of the regularly organised exhibitions.

Similarly, in Paris, one can see the spectacular strong room of the central branch of the Société Générale bank (see "Secret Paris" by the same publisher).

TO SEE NEARBY
THE SUNDIAL OF THE NEW CHURCH (NIEUWE KERK)
Above the wing of the New Church on the Dam Square side is a sundial, from which all the town clocks were calibrated up until 1880.

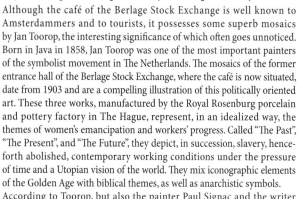

TO SEE NEARBY

THE SYMBOLIST PAINTINGS OF THE 'BERLAGE' STOCK EXCHANGE CAFÉ 26
Beurs van Berlage Café, Damrak 277, 1012ZJ Amsterdam
- Tel.: 020 530 41 41
- Open Monday till Saturday 10am till 6pm, Sunday 11am till 6pm

Although the café of the Berlage Stock Exchange is well known to Amsterdammers and to tourists, it possesses some superb mosaics by Jan Toorop, the interesting significance of which often goes unnoticed. Born in Java in 1858, Jan Toorop was one of the most important painters of the symbolist movement in The Netherlands. The mosaics of the former entrance hall of the Berlage Stock Exchange, where the café is now situated, date from 1903 and are a compelling illustration of this politically oriented art. These three works, manufactured by the Royal Rosenburg porcelain and pottery factory in The Hague, represent, in an idealized way, the themes of women's emancipation and workers' progress. Called "The Past", "The Present", and "The Future", they depict, in succession, slavery, henceforth abolished, contemporary working conditions under the pressure of time and a Utopian vision of the world. They mix iconographic elements of the Golden Age with biblical themes, as well as anarchistic symbols.

According to Toorop, but also the painter Paul Signac and the writer William Morris, the Golden Age is not to be sought in the past but in the future, which remains to be defined and constructed. Jan Toorop was in the process of converting from anarchism to Catholicism at the time he produced these mosaics. The representation of Christ and the Samaritan by the Well is thus a Catholic illustration of a future possible for all, regardless of condition. If Berlage and Toorop represented a liberal left that did not call for revolution, these pictures, which certainly created tension between their socialist ideals and the capitalist functions of the Stock Exchange, were misunderstood. The brokers demanded, in vain, that they be removed.

JAN TOOROOP AND THE SYMBOLIST MOVEMENT IN THE NETHERLANDS
Symbolism was a literary and artistic movement that appeared in France and Belgium around 1880, in reaction to an all too materialistic world, resulting from the industrial revolution and technical progress, from the rise of capitalism and the class struggle. In the spirit of the end of the century, the themes developed by the symbolists were expectation, lethargy, melancholy and desire for change. Rather dreamers or Utopians, the symbolist artists were pioneers of modernism, exploring the very recent Freudian concept of the subconscious, while seeking to achieve the Beautiful. Emblematic, rather than religious or mythological, they used symbols as a metaphorical language. This movement found its origins in the French poetry of Arthur Rimbaud, Paul Verlaine and Stéphane Mallarmé, and in Belgium with Emile Verhaeren and Maurice Maeterlinck. This cultural movement subsequently extended to painting and the theatre, influencing art throughout Europe. Among painters, one musn't forget the Belgian Fernand Khnopff or Jan Toorop, the most renowned Dutch symbolist.

TO SEE NEARBY

HUGO KAAGMAN'S GRAFFITI
Centraal Station, quai 2b

On platform 2b of the Central Station are 72 compositions by Hugo Kaagman, inspired by Delft Blue tiles, but with modern, provocative motifs. A rather ironic commentary on political life and contemporary events, this graffiti has been called "shocking blue". One can see, for example, a play on words: "2b or not 2b", the famous phrase from Shakespeare's Hamlet. Hugo Kaagman developed his own style of graffiti from 1969 and became well known for his work at the beginning of 1980s. Using stencils and aerosol paint, his designs use repeated motifs, which also appear in mirror image.

THE HOUSES SET INTO THE VICTORIA HOTEL ㉘
Prins Hendrikkade 47, 1012TM Amsterdam

Opposite the Central Station, the enormous building of the Victoria Hotel, a grand hotel built of dressed stone between 1883 and 1890, surrounds two tiny 17th century houses. They are easy to locate as one has a souvenir shop based on the ground floor. The proprietor, an elderly woman, quite simply refused to sell them when the hotel was built.

These houses date from 1602, although the descriptive plaque of No 47 indicates a reconstruction in 1648. At the time, these houses were built very low, so that the houses along the Damrak could also enjoy an attractive rear view onto the harbour.

THE WINGED WHEELS OF THE CENTRAL STATION ㉙
On the roof of the hall of the Central Station

The symbol of the Dutch Railways is a winged wheel: a locomotive wheel with large wings attached to the axle symbolizing the god of commerce, Mercury. From 1889, two very large wheels of more than 5m in diameter had been situated at the highest point of the Central Station hall. Around 1930 the wheels were taken down, as they had become so rusty they risked crashing down. More than 75 years later they have found their place again.

THE GABLE STONE OF THE "IN DE WILDEMAN" BAR ㉚
Gable stone, Nieuwezijds Voorburgwal 45-47, 1012RD Amsterdam
Tasting bar In de Wildeman, Kolksteeg 3, 1012PT Amsterdam
• Tel.: 020 638 23 48
• Open Monday to Saturday 12pm till 1am, Friday and Saturday till 2am

At No 45 Nieuwezijds Voorburgwal, an amusing gable stone represents a savage or "Wildeman", whose attributes are both mythical - a lion's skin in the manner of Hercules - and heraldic - the garland of oak leaves on the hip.

This plaque provided the name for the tasting bar of the Levert & Co distillery, which was founded in 1690. This authentic venue has retained the charm of former ages and offers more than 200 different bottled beers and almost 20 on draft.

SINTER CLAES

THE GABLE STONE OF SAINT NICHOLAS   ㉛

Dam 2, 1012 JS Amsterdam

> *Saint Nicholas, the holy protector of Amsterdam and patron saint of sailors, unmarried young girls and butchers*

In former times, a market named after St Nicholas was held on Dam Square. Here a fine gable stone can be seen; it illustrates one of the legends of this Saint, who is highly regarded by the Dutch - that of three rich but unfortunate young people. In the course of a pilgrimage, they were robbed and killed by an innkeeper. He supposedly cut them up in pieces, which he salted in a barrel. Seven years later, St Nicholas came to the inn.

Asking for meat to eat, he was given a piece of human flesh. Recognizing the young people, he brought them back to life. One can find traces of a house named after St Nicholas dating from 1564. The gable stone certainly dates from that era, even though it is now mounted on a 17th century house.

THE OTHER LEGENDS OF ST NICHOLAS

Nicholas, the Bishop of Myra (in what is today Turkey), was born around 270 AD and died on 6 December 340. He plays an important role in The Netherlands and particularly in Amsterdam. St Nicholas is not only the holy protector of Amsterdam, he is also the patron Saint of sailors, hence the representation of him with a small boat. According to legend, he appeared to sailors begging for his help during a storm and calmed the water for them. He is also the protector of unmarried young girls and butchers.

These attributions are linked to 10th century legends. During a voyage he was making to the Holy Land, a storm suddenly arose. It only took a prayer by St Nicholas for the storm to abate. At Patara, in the south of Turkey, there lived a noble man with three daughters, but he was too poor to provide them with dowries. The girls had to earn a living and their only option was prostitution. When Nicholas, still a young boy, passed their window one night he saw them weeping. The three following nights, he threw them a small sack of gold coins. The girls could then marry men of their own rank. St Nicholas became "Sinterklaas" after the Alteration (see page 25), to avoid using the word "Saint".

In the Rijksmuseum, don't miss the famous painting of the Feast of St Nicholas, by Jan Steen. On the table in the right foreground you'll see some gold coins, an allusion to the legend of St Nicholas as the protector of young unmarried girls.

THE SECRET CHAPEL OF THE PARROT

Church of Saint Peter and Saint Paul
Papegaai Kapel, Kalverstraat 58, 1012PG Amsterdam
Second entrance: Nieuwezijds Voorburgwal 293,
• Tel.: 020 623 18 89
• Open every day, 10am till 6pm. Mass on weekdays at 10:30am.
• High Mass Sunday morning 10:30am and 12:15pm,
in Latin with Gregorian chants

"A quarter of an hour for God"

Even though one can easily pass by it innumerable times without noticing it, the Chapel of the Parrot, with its eye-catching slogan "a quarter of an hour for God", is certainly worth the detour. The Chapel of Saint Joseph, its official name, was built by the Jesuit priest Augustus van Teylingen in the gardens of a house that belonged, it is said, to a bird-seller. The gable stone of this house was decorated with a parrot to indicate the shop's location. Indeed, at the end of the church, in the choir, is a polychrome painted on an oak panel, representing a parrot, which would have been used as the shop's street display. Out of love for the bird, the first priest Willem Willemart finally gave the chapel the nickname "The Parrot". Built in 1672, after the Alteration, the chapel was originally a secret chapel. Its façade on the street is very narrow, providing no hint of the extensive building behind it.

In 1848 the chapel was entirely renovated in a Neo-Gothic style by the architect G. Moele. An official entrance was added, notable for an interesting façade decorated with glazed ceramics. It was then given the name "The church of Saint Peter and Saint Paul".

After the Alteration, Catholic churches were often known by a code name. It could be linked to an animal, as here with "the parrot", or "de duif" (church of the dove, Prinsengracht 756), or to an event like the Church of the Miracle, or even by an allusion to the building itself, like "ons lieve Heer op solder" ("the good Lord in the attic", Oudezijds Voorburgwal 40).

1 3 45

GEDACHTENIS TER
HEILIGE STEDE

COMMEMORATION OF THE AMSTERDAM MIRACLE ㉝

Kalverstraat 81, 1012PA Amsterdam
• Opposite the entrance of the Amsterdam Museum

> **The miracle of Amsterdam, at the origin of the arms of the Imperial crown**

A t No 81 Kalverstraat, a stone was set into the wall of what was once the Holy Chapel or "Heilige Stede" constructed to mark the miracle of Amsterdam.

On 15 March 1345, a miracle occurred at the house of the Dommer family, who lived at the corner of the Wijdekapel. Mr. Ijsbrand Dommer was very ill and had the priest called to give him the last rites. The latter gave him the Last Communion. Shortly after, Mr. Dommer vomited violently into a bucket and his wife emptied it onto the fire. The following morning, Ijsbrand had passed away but the white Host was still intact in the middle of the flames, miraculously preserved.

The Heilige Stede was built on the same spot. This chapel welcomed countless pilgrims, and gave the name Holy Way or "Heilige weg" to the street which led to this chapel from Sloten, a village to the west of Amsterdam. The street between the Kalverstraat and the Singel has kept this name.

1489 marked another episode in the history of the miracle. The daughter of Maximilian of Austria was very ill. Since the death of his wife in 1482, Maximilian had been regent of his son Philip The Handsome, who had inherited the Low Countries. In a final attempt to find a cure for his daughter, Maximilian brought her to Amsterdam, to the chapel of the miracle. She was cured and, by way of thanks, the Emperor gave the town of Amsterdam the right to insert the Imperial Crown into its arms.

Interpretations vary on the reason for this protection. Some say it was actually to thank The Netherlands for having lent money to the House of Austria. Others say it was simply gratitude, his sick daughter having been healed after her visit to the chapel of the Amsterdam miracle.

After the alteration (see page 25), as the chapel had became protestant, the Roman Catholics moved into a hidden chapel in the Begijnhof and took over the story of the miracle through illustrations in the glass windows and on paintings (see page 77).

Every year, in memory of the Amsterdam miracle, a procession takes place in the early morning one day in March. Several thousand pilgrims of all religions take part in this procession that starts and finishes at the gable stone of No 81 Kalverstraat.

THE GABLE STONES OF THE PROFESSIONS:
A TESTIMONIAL OF THE OCCUPATIONS OF THE 19TH CENTURY

The city centre and the Jordaan neighbourhood host numerous gable stones that reflect in one way or another the trades of their former owners. They can be the perfect excuse for a pleasurable stroll.

Close to the Amsterdam Museum (Nieuwezijds Voorburgwal 357), going towards the Saint-Lucien Alley (Sint Luciënsteeg), is a wall where no less than 47 gable stones were gathered in 1924. Note the wheat porter from 1626 (Corendrager), the milk-maid (Het melkmeisje), and the representation of a tooth for the dentist.

As you stroll about in the centre, you can spot the slaughterhouse inspectors (Oudezijds Voorburgwal 274), the surveyor with his plumb line (Spuistraat 295), the peat gatherer (Turfdraagsterpad) and the wheat cutter (Bethaniëndwarsstraat 18).

If you stroll through the Jordaan, you will find the shepherd (Haarlemmerdijk 98), the glazier (Driehoekstraat 4), and a man calculating the wheat crop (Brouwersgracht 163). Heading south, you will see the brewer (Egelantiersgracht 8), the young carpenter (Egelantiersgracht 15), the hand of the public writer (Egelantiersgracht 52), the tailor (Egelantiersgracht 89), the nanny (Nieuwe Leliestraat 82), the town crier (Bloemstraat 12), the sowers (Bloemgracht 77 & 81), the baker (Eerste Tuindwarsstraat 19) and, finally, the two blacksmiths (Lauriergracht 5).

DE TVRFVVLSTER

ANNO   De Jonge Saaijer   1763

WHERE DO THE GABLE STONES COME FROM ?

Usually located at mid-height of the façade, these picturesque carved stones date back from the time when streets did not usually have an official name, houses did not have numbers and most people could not read.

These stones, decorated with a drawing, a little scene, a heraldic device or a motto, were used as marker points in the city.

It is only since 1806, thanks to the reforms of Louis Bonaparte, that Amsterdam, like most places in Europe, has used the numbering system of streets with even and odd numbers.

The lowest numbers are closest to Centraal station.

Today, there are still close to 600 old gable stones in Amsterdam. They have been preserved and in some cases renovated.

Most of them are on their original gables but some have been moved, when, for example, a building or a complete neighbourhood had to be rebuilt.

Saved from demolition, they have been gathered on one wall, creating a small open-air museum.

On the wall of the St Olofssteeg alley, which opens onto the Zeedijk, there are several gable stones saved from demolished houses in this neighbourhood.

THE PIGEONHOLES OF THE ORPHANS

In the Amsterdam Museum
Kalverstraat 92, 1012PH Amsterdam
• Tel.: 020 530 17 44
• Open Monday to Friday 10am till 7pm, Saturday, Sunday and public holidays 11am till 7pm

A cloister turned into an orphanage

Located within the Museum of Amsterdam, the old Saint Lucien's cloister is a much-appreciated stop for visitors. You gain access via the narrow Saint Lucien Alley or "Sint Luciensteeg", or from the Kalverstraat, by passing under a lovely archway in sculpted stone. After the Reformation in 1581, Saint Lucien monastery was transformed into a public orphanage. Evidence of this can be seen in the decorated tympanum depicting young children dressed in red and black, the colours of the city of Amsterdam. They are grouped around a dove, the symbol of The Holy Spirit. This tympanum is a copy, as the original is located at the entry of the museum.

Here, one can also read a text from the poet Vondel, inciting people to be charitable: "Wij groeien vast in tal en last, ons tweede vaders klagen; Ay, ga niet voort door deze poort, of help een luttel dragen." ("We are more and more numerous and our adoptive fathers are complaining, so don't pass this door without giving a few pence"). On the right is a bronze urn into which passers-by were invited to put their alms. The complex was renovated in the 17th century by Jacob van Campen and continued to be an orphanage until 1960. Nowadays, the Museum café Mokum is installed in what used to be the stables. Opposite on the right, the building that remains is where the little orphan boys lived. Opposite on the left, one can see the wooden pigeonholes where they kept their working clothes and tools, until they reached the age to depart to apprenticeships. Today, these pigeonholes are often used for exhibitions. The town Museum is situated in what was the girls' orphanage. From the entrance one can see, after asking for permission, on the right, the room of the Regents, where decisions were taken in council.

WHY ARE THE PAVING STONES OF THE ORPHANAGE COURTYARD YELLOW ?
The courtyard is paved with little yellow stones. From 1672, this colour was, in fact, reserved for private lanes, to prevent people from using red paving stones from the public streets to repair their own lanes.

Between the boys' orphanage and the girls' orphanage there used to be a ditch or "sloot", which surrounded the entire former Saint Lucien monastery until 1865. It has since been filled in and the street that replaced it is called "Gedempte sloot". Today, it houses a covered gallery, open to the public, where one can admire paintings of the civic guard companies dating from the 16th, 17th and 18th centuries.

TO SEE NEARBY

HAJENIUS ART DECO TOBACCO SHOP

35

P.G.C. Hajenius, Rokin 92-96, 1012KZ Amsterdam
• Tel.: 020 623 74 94 • Open Monday 12pm till 6pm, Tuesday to Saturday
9:30am till 6pm, Sunday 12pm till 5pm

Founded originally in 1826, the Hajenius tobacco shop has boasted a superb
Art Deco décor, classed as a historical monument, for more than a century.
Possessed of a strong business sense and passionate about cigars, Pantaleon
Gerhard Coenraad Hajenius started his first cigar and tobacco shop when
he was only 19 years old. He opened it next door to the Rijnstroom hotel
on the Dam square, a most desirable location in a prosperous area close to
the tobacco exchange and to about 30 small cigar makers.

He had cigars produced from the best tobacco, and sold them under his own
name. In 1868, because of road works to widen the street, he was obliged to
move and set up his shop afresh, this time on the Dam, where the Peek &
Cloppenburg shop is now located. His reputation was made, and his cigars
became famous far and wide, even beyond the national borders, winning
medals and diplomas at international exhibitions. The House of Hajenius
even became the official supplier to several European Courts.

Such was the firm's prosperity that it moved again in 1914, to larger premises.
The new store was on the Rokin and mirrored its success with a dressed
stone exterior and a superb Art Deco interior, the style in vogue at that
time. The design was entrusted to the Van Gendt brothers, architects who
became famous particularly for the construction of the Concert Gebouw,
in a Neo-Renaissance style.

The Royal Crown is sculpted above the entrance, as the tobacco shop was
one of the official suppliers to the Royal Household (see page 175). On the
façade the name "the Rijnstroom" can still be seen; it was retained, despite
the relocations. Inside, note in particular the Italian marble on the walls and
counters, the crafted bronzes and the splendid brass chandeliers, which were
originally lit by gas. The tobacco jars on the shelves are of Delft pottery.

This shop has a high reputation amongst cigar lovers, particularly because
of its attention to temperature and humidity controls. Keeping cigars in a
perfect state was of profound importance in the construction of the premises,
even to an absence of paint to avoid the mixing of odors.

**ON DEMAND, CIGARS FROM YOUR OWN PERSONAL COLLECTION CAN BE
DELIVERED BY SPECIAL MESSENGER...**

Cigar lovers will appreciate the cigar bar, the library and a small
museum. For the very well-to-do, there is also an air-conditioned
strong-room, and, on demand, cigars from one's personal collection
are delivered by a messenger.

As indicated on page 175, to become a "hofleverancier", a business
has to be Dutch, which hasn't been the case with Hajenius since 1978.
But, here, the Royal Arms remain above the entrance because they
are an integral part of the wall and cannot be removed.

THE GABLE STONE OF THE UNCUT DIAMOND
Rokin 130, 1012ND Amsterdam

This stone plaque represents a rough octagonal diamond, indicating that it is uncut. The inscription uses the words "de rovwe diamant", meaning 'uncut diamond' in Old Dutch. This plaque was recently restored in full colour.

AMSTERDAM: THE FORMER WORLD DIAMOND CAPITAL

For centuries Amsterdam was the diamond capital of the world. From the harbour, ships of the Dutch East India Company (V.O.C.) followed the route traced by Vasco da Gama in 1498 to bring back spices and diamonds from the East Indies.

The town of Amsterdam developed as a diamond centre following Venice, Bruges and Antwerp, thanks to the arrival of Sephardic Jews after 1578. Leaving the intolerant Spain of Philip II, many of them found refuge in Amsterdam. As diamond cutting was not regulated by a guild, they were allowed to practice their craft. Traces have been found, from 1586, of one of the first diamond cutters, Willem Vermaet.

In 1725, a Portuguese man discovered the first diamonds in Brazil, but, thanks to relations maintained by the Jews with the Iberian Peninsula, The Netherlands were able to negotiate a concession with the Portuguese Crown to intensively exploit the output of the Brazilian mines. The trading and cutting of diamonds developed until the end of the 18th century, when an arrangement between the London banker Henry Hope and the Portuguese mine owners in Brazil led to the transfer of the uncut diamond business to London. Amsterdam nevertheless held on to its position as a grand centre of diamond cutting and the cut-diamond trade. The intensive exploitation of the Brazilian diamond layers ended, however, in a sharp fall in production. The diamond business went into a long recession towards the middle of the 19th century.

Prosperity returned with the discovery of diamonds at Kimberly in South Africa in the 1870s. Several years later, the diamond business had regained its earlier dimension: it was the famous "Cape" era. But the high cost of skilled man-power and the power of the unions gradually led to the decline of Amsterdam, to the benefit of Antwerp, the Belgian diamond centre. But it was finally the German occupation during World War Two that precipitated the collapse of the Amsterdam diamond industry. Many Jews had chosen to work in this industry since the 17th century, as other crafts were controlled by Guilds, to which they had no access. Of the 2000 members of the diamond exchange, only 20% escaped the Holocaust.

Several families returned, like the van Moppes who had fled to Brazil, and other names like Stoeltie, Slijper, Asscher (see page 249), Coster and Gassan proved that all had not completely disappeared. Nevertheless, today only the latter two of these families still play an important role in the diamond industry. A final strike, lasting more than 13 weeks, signalled the end of this industry in 1953. Amsterdam is today of minor importance as a diamond centre, but remains known for its diamond cutters. Today, only two big diamond cutting centres remain open to the public, although the visit is very touristy: Gassan (Nieuwe Uilenburgerstraat 173-175, 1011LN Amsterdam) and Coster Diamonds (Paulus Potterstraat 2-6, 1071CZ Amsterdam).

THE TOMBSTONE OF CORNELIA ARENTS ③⑦

Next to the English Church of the Begjinhof
- Entry from Spuistraat or Gedempte Begijnensloot
- Open between 8am and 5pm (no groups)
- Please respect the calm of this private place

> **Buried in the gutter**

In a small corner of this lovely square, one can easily pass by this stone marker, near the pavement on a low wall. However, this marker is a good illustration of the sometimes difficult co-habitation of the Christian faiths - Catholic and Protestant.

From 1150, the Convent, or "Begijnhof," was inhabited by pious unmarried Catholic women. While the church situated in its centre is one of the oldest in Amsterdam, it is nevertheless no longer Catholic: in 1578, at the time of the Alteration, the nuns had to relinquish it to the city, who gave it 30 years later to the English Reformed Church. They took refuge in the houses at Nos 29-31, and transformed them into a secret church. Even today this church holds Catholic services, including a mass in French. Between the English Church and the lawn, on the side nearest the Begijnensloot, there are several slightly different stones. They mark the tombstone of Cornelia Arents, a superior of the Convent, who died on 2 May 1654, as mentioned on the stone mounted on the low wall.

This pure and hard-line Catholic refused to go along with her family's conversion to Protestantism and preferred to be buried "in the gutter" than in the Protestant Church. In 1655 her wish was granted and her remains were moved to the exterior of the church.

Each year on 2 May, homage is paid to this principled woman by the placing of flowers on her tomb.

TO SEE NEARBY

BILINGUAL PLAQUES ③⑧

On the het Spui Square, between the stalls of booksellers, there are three pairs of chiselled plaques at ground level. On these plaques, one can read the text "translation from one language to another" in several colours and four languages. This project was created in 1996 by Lawrence Weiner, an American from the Bronx and a pioneer of conceptual art. The artist wanted to illustrate that reading allows access to knowledge.

TO SEE NEARBY

THE STATUE OF THE LITTLE AMSTERDAM BOY

The statue called "Het Lieverdje" or "The little Darling", situated on the het Spui Square, represents a small boy who once fished a drowning dog out of a canal. In fact, it pays tribute to the street urchins of Amsterdam, big-hearted little rascals. This tribute was organized by Henri Knap, who wrote a column on local life in the great Amsterdam daily paper, Het Parool. Financed by an Eindhoven cigarette manufacturer, this bronze statue was sculpted by Carel Kneulman (1915-2008), an artist linked to the Cobra movement. It was inaugurated on 10 September 1960 by the mayor's wife. For four years it remained the symbol of the altruism of Amsterdammers. Then, during the summer of 1964, it became the meeting place of rebellious youth; the instigator, Robert Jasper Grootveld, self-proclaimed anti-smoke magician, used the statue as the backdrop for his open-air theatre (see below).

THE PROVO MOVEMENT

The Provo movement came to life in Amsterdam in the 1960s in reaction to the system, notably the monarchy and the ignorance of the masses. It was a political and cultural movement, with anarchistic tendencies, and owed its name to the revue "Provokatie". Its first issue, dated 12 July 1965, included pseudo-instructions on how to make a bomb from acorns, which caused it to be censured.

This movement has left memories of its artistic manifestations, including the famous "Saturday evening happenings" around Het Lieverdje statue on het Spui. On the political side, the Provos challenged people's beliefs through Utopian propositions, called white schemes, whose aim was to make life simpler and more sound.

Thus the scheme for white housing, a precursor of the squatting movement, proposed the right to occupy empty accommodation. The best-known scheme was that of the white bikes - bikes for free use, with no padlocks, to liberate people from cars. More innovative, the white children scheme had the aim of breaking down barriers by proposing that couples share the responsibility for looking after others' children one day a week in addition to their own. The white chimney scheme proposed a tax on those who polluted the air.

From 1966, the movement lined up with activists: pamphlets were thrown from a bridge on to the boat of Princes Beatrix, who was on an outing with her fiancé Prins Claus von Amsberg, a German whose unpopularity was linked to his enrolment in the German army in 1944.

Several months later, smoke bombs were hurled into the middle of their wedding procession, provoking an incident that was reported worldwide. The institutionalization of the movement reached its peak in the election of Bernhard de Vries, representative of the Provos in the Amsterdam municipal elections of June 1966. Having become "too structured", the movement preferred to dissolve itself at its last "happening" in the Vondelpark in May 1967.

THE DOORWAY OF THE RASPHUIS PRISON ⓵

Heiligeweg 19, 1012XN Amsterdam

When the prisoners rasped Brazilian wood

Of the old Rasphuis or "Rasping House", only its superb doorway remains, designed in 1603 by Hendrick de Keyser. Today, it seems a bit lost in the middle of a busy shopping area.

Until 1578, this was the site of the Convent of the Poor Clares, which, like all the convents and monasteries, was closed after the Alteration (see page 25). In 1598, the town council decided to establish a house of correction here, in response to the ideas of Dirck Volkertsz. Coomhert, and in 1696 the Rasphuis was built.

Those sent here were for the most part young men who had broken the law. They had to rasp Brazilian wood with a rasp containing from 8 to 12 blades. The powder obtained was destined for the colour industry, were it was mixed with water, and then, after oxidation and reduction, transformed into pigment that was used in paint or textile dyes. On the doorway can be seen decorations illustrating the history of the place - a wood cart drawn by wild animals being chastised by the carter. Above can be read a proverb from Seneca, "Virtutis est domare quae cuncti pavent" ("It is virtuous to subdue the one everyone fears"). Note also the symbol of Discipline, "Castigatio", represented by a woman with a chained man on either side of her.

Any prisoner who didn't want to work was shut up in a cellar that was below sea level.
The prisoner had a hand-pump at his disposal and thus had to choose between pumping and drowning, hence the Dutch expression "pompen of verzuipen" ("pump or drown").

WALKING IN SEARCH OF BIBLICAL GABLE STONES

There were more than 20 monasteries in Amsterdam in the Middle Ages. Today, one can begin an interesting tour at the Begijnhof in search of gable stones related to the Bible.

On the wall on the left when you enter from het Spui Square, you can see a lovely series of gable stones that were collected here in 1961. From the Old Testament, you can recognize, from top to bottom and from left to right: Jacob's door, Elias fed by the crows (Kings. 17:4-6) dating from 1601, the sacrifice of Abraham (Gen.22:10-13) and Daniel and his friends thrown into the furnace (Dan.3:25).

From the New Testament are Jesus the Saviour (In de Salvaeter) and an allegory of Faith (Het Geloof), then the flight from Egypt (Mat.2:12-15) and the disciples on the road to Emmaus (Luke.24:15-35). At number 19 in the Begijnhof, you can also see another gable stone in monochrome illustrating the flight out of Egypt. Going north to the Dam, stop in front of Moses separating the waters (Nieuwezijds Voorburgwal 117), then another flight out of Egypt (Nieuwezijds Voorburgwal 29) and Elias fed by the crows (Dirk van Hasseltsteeg 51). Farther along, on the Oudekerksplein, behind the Oude Kerk church, is a plaque of the Annunciation (Luke.1:26-38) dating from 1571. You can also see the dance of the golden calf (Exodus 32:19) at Lange Niezel 25 and Noah's Ark on the wall of the Oudezijds Kolk. Heading in the direction of the canals, at Langestraat 30, you will find an interesting gable stone featuring Job. The inscription D.G.I. means « de Gedulige Iob » (Job the accursed). Farther, at Binnen Brouwersstraat 22, you can find the miraculous harvest of fish. Pass along Prinsengracht 159-171 to see the lovely multi-coloured Noah's ark. Continuing towards the north of the Jordaan, note King David at Vinkenstraat 1, and then don't miss the splendid gable stone of the multiplication of loaves on Binnen Dommersstraat 13-15.

ABRAHAM

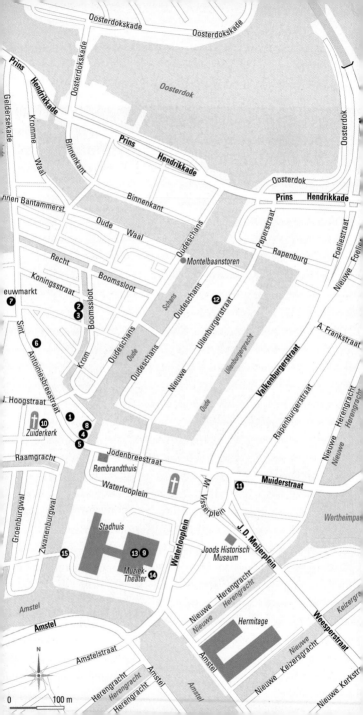

CENTRE - JEWISH QUARTER

THE CEILINGS OF THE PINTO HOUSE

Pinto Huis, Sint Antoniesbreestraat 69, 1011HB Amsterdam
• Open Monday, Wednesday and Friday 10am-5:30pm,
and Saturday 11am-4pm

A little-known jewel

Named after the rich Pinto family, this imposing classical style house today contains a public library with little-known superbly painted ceilings.

Fleeing the inquisition against the Jews in Portugal, the Da Pinto family immigrated to The Netherlands at the very beginning of the 17th century. They set themselves up as bankers, initially in Antwerp, then in Rotterdam and finally in Amsterdam. They gradually amassed a considerable fortune, which gave rise to the expression "rich as a Pinto". Their friendship with the Stadhouder William IV led to their financing the war with France.

In 1651, Isaac de Pinto, one of the descendants, bought the building at No 69 Sint Antoniesbreestraat. It was not situated beside a canal, as were the majority of the houses of the wealthy, and benefited from a wider frontage than the canal-side dwellings. His son, David Emmanuel, reconstructed the house entirely in the 1680s in an imposing classical style; architect Elias Bouwman designed the impressive dressed stone façade.

The house stayed in the family till the 19th century but was then abandoned. In the early 1970s the building was threatened with demolition and was purchased by the city. After several years of contesting fast highway and metro projects, the house was finally restored in 1975.

Because the Pinto house has been converted into a public library, one can easily admire the rich vaulted period ceilings, in particular the cherubs, birds and floral decorations by the famous 17th century master Jacob de Wit.

The painter Th. Kurpershoek restored the paintings at the end of the 20th century but, as some panels had been lost, he took the opportunity to create new ones. These are easily recognizable by the glimpses of contemporary life which have been slipped in: building work on the house, people on bikes, a glass bottle… one can spot the presence of a little angel who is reading, a reminder of the current use of the building.

The decoration of the ceiling panel in the corridor, representing a sky with birds, is a replica created with the aid of photos, the original having been stolen when the house was abandoned. In one of the rooms towards the rear, one can see seven paintings by Nicolas Wijnberg. In the painting in the centre, there are four moons belonging to the coat of arms of the Pinto family. The floral decorations on the beams are authentic.

TO SEE NEARBY

THE OLD WAREHOUSES OF THE KROMBOOMSSLOOT ❷
Kromboomssloot 18-20, 1011GW Amsterdam

Kromboomssloot is a picturesque canal, a little bit off the beaten track, where time seems to stand still. In the Middle Ages, this zone was the industrial area of Lastage, a name linked to the verbs 'lasten', to load and 'ontlasten', to unload. It was brought within the town walls of Amsterdam in 1585. Ships were brought into these yards for repair before long voyages. There used to be caulking yards for boats here, as well as mast and rope makers. The latter needed great spaces to stretch out the hemp fibres. Some of them belonged to the rope maker and shipbuilder Cornelis Pietersz. Boom. The water flowed alongside his land, from which derived the name Kromboomssloot, a contraction of Cornelis Boom z'n Sloot or ditch.

Along what is now a very pretty canal, on the building at numbers 61-63, dating from 1757, a tiger is depicted. It is on the rear façade of a merchant's house, or "Koopmanshuis", on the neighbouring canal Oude Schans, whose cornice decoration represents a tiger.

Don't fail to notice the very fine example of a double warehouse, dating from 1636, at number 18-20, which is equipped with a most exceptional windlass in the loft. This warehouse carries the name "De Schottenburg" or the "Scottish Bastion", from the former wool trade with Scotland. Renovated in 1979, this lovely building has been turned into apartments.

THE WINDING MECHANISMS IN THE LOFTS OR "WINDASKASTEN" ❸
Kromboomssloot 18-20 (1636), Herengracht 502
Keizersgracht 40-44 (1600), Prins Hendrikkade 176

On the old warehouses of Kromboomssloot, one can see a sort of cupboard integrated into the façade. This protects an ingenious and rare haulage mechanism: on the exterior, the mechanism comprises a rope with a hook on the end to which goods to be hauled up were fixed. This rope passed through a pulley, on the end of the hoisting beam, before entering the loft. In the interior of the loft, the winding mechanism was akin to that in a windmill with a reduction gear. Sometimes the ropes extended from the loft to lower floors, even to the ground floor, through slots in the ceiling. Such is the case with the mechanism at No 502 Herengracht. This house was bequeathed by Cornelis van Aalst, in 1926, to the Town Hall of Amsterdam and has since been used by the Mayor to host functions.

THE LEPERS' DOORWAY AND THEIR RATTLE ❹

Sint Antoniesluis 24, 1011 JB Amsterdam

*A doorway
that moves*

I ntegrated into a modern building, the Lepers' doorway is an anachronistic relic that has miraculously survived the test of time. The doorway marked the entry of the Lazarus, a lepers' house built in the 15th century, which was then outside the town, on the dike which led to Muiden, the site now called Mr. Visserplein. The door itself dates from the renovation of the lepers' house around 1609. Built in dressed stone, its resemblance to the doorway of the Zuiderkerk gives grounds for thinking that its design came from the studios of Hendrick de Keyser and that perhaps the sculptor Nicholas Stone created it. Lepers used a rattle in order to alert other people of their approach, so that they could walk away and avoid contagion.

In the 1860s the lepers' house was demolished to make way for a police station. A century later, the door itself was dismantled to allow the building of the tunnel under the river IJ. Thanks to the Pinto Foundation, the stones of the doorway were reassembled as they had been and integrated into a wall behind the Pinto house, only a few metres from their original location.

The high reliefs were carved later, about 1975, by the sculptor Henry van Haaren to replace those that had disappeared. They depict a man and a woman, both lepers, the man holding a rattle. By opening the door, a pretty little court-yard can be seen, in front of a brick house on the left, which is none other than the rear of the Pinto house (see preceding double page).

TO SEE NEARBY

AMSTERDAM, AT THE CENTRE OF THE WORLD ❺

Opposite the tortoise of the boundary column (see following page), looking towards the Oude Schans canal, one's attention is naturally drawn to the Montelbaan tower and to the lock which regulated the entry of seawater into the canals up until the 1930s. Even so, on the footpath on the bridge of the Sint Antoniesluis, don't overlook a map of the world, plus a map of Amsterdam with the River Amstel, in marble.

Here one can observe that Moscow is 2150 km to the East of Amsterdam and Mecca 4550 km to the southeast. It just goes to show that, wherever one calls home, pride makes one believe that one is at the centre of the world.

TO SEE NEARBY

THE TREE OF LIFE AND THE CRADLE SONG OF THE J.W. SIEBBELESHOFJE ⑥
J.W. Siebbeleshof, 1011DC Amsterdam

The Siebbeleshofje is situated behind the Kromboomssloot and extends ▶
parallel to Sint Antoniesbreestraat.

Just behind the busy square of the Nieuwmarkt, the Siebbeleshofje was
constructed on the site of the former Rotterdammersloot canal, which
was filled in in 1867 as it was insalubrious. After the Second World War,
new buildings were constructed. In the middle of this modern court, a big
12-meter pylon in blueish stone represents a tree of life. Put up in 1989, it
is one of the best-known works of the artist Wim Tap. The stone symbolises
the fossilization of fish at the bottom of the sea, creating the earth and the
landscape, a mix of illusion and reality.

The ground of this court is also embellished with dozens of paving stones,
each marked with a letter. These form several verses of a cradle song by
the poet Hans Andreus (1926-1977) paying tribute to the women sitting in
the windows of this red-light district.

THE MESSAGE ON THE PLATFORM OF THE NIEUWMARKT METRO STATION ⑦
On the tiled floor of the Nieuwmarkt Metro Station, each of the large tiles is
inscribed with one of the letters of a slogan "wonen is geen gunst maar een
recht", meaning "housing is not a favour it's a right".

This phrase recalls the debates of the years around 1975, when numerous
houses in this area were demolished to make way for the construction of
the subway.

THE COLUMN OF THE BOUNDARY LINES ⑧
Sint Antoniesluis 24, 1011JB Amsterdam

On Jodenbreestraat, opposite
the Sluyswacht café, a rather
surprising column attracts one's
attention. Called the column of
the boundary lines or "Grenspaal"
it was created by the artist Hans 't
Mannetje in 1968 and symbolises
the boundary between the old
part and the renovated part of
the neighbourhood. It is a tribute
to the people of this neighbourhood who stood against its
destruction in the 1960s.

Its base comprises a stone tortoise
and a carved poem by Jacob Israël
de Haan, which tells about the
nostalgia of the Jews who moved
from here to Jerusalem.

TO SEE NEARBY

THE STATUE OF THE VIOLINIST **9**
Muziektheater Hallway, Waterlooplein 22, 1011PG Amsterdam
This rather startling statue by an unknown artist dates from 1991. A violin player seems to hatch out of the ground, breaking the marble flooring like a baby bird breaking out of its shell. Enjoy the little poem "muziek rijst op" extolling music.

THE WATERFALL BUILDING **10**
Zuiderkerkhof, 1011WB Amsterdam
• Does not operate during cold weather

Situated in a quiet courtyard, in which some might see the Piazza del Campo in Sienna in miniature, this modern building (1983) by the architect Hans Hagenbeek, has an amusing fountain: the big bay window serves as the back-wall of a waterfall. Although the white marble basin is regularly defaced by graffiti, this creation is very decorative, particularly when the sunlight throws the reflection of the Zuiderkerk tower on to the stone base beneath the stream of water.

PANORAMA FROM THE TOWER OF THE ZUIDERKERK (SOUTH CHURCH)
During summer, it is possible to climb the tower of the South Church. This tower is surmounted by the royal crown and was added 3 years after the construction of the church. The Hemony brothers cast its carillon bells in 1656 (see page 61).

Although there is no proof, Rembrandt, who lived 100 metres away at No 3 Jodenbreestraat, now the Rembrandt museum, may well have used the vast space of the Zuiderkerk as his workshop for the production of his monumental painting The Night Watch in 1642.

The Muziektheater building stands where the Jewish ghetto was during the Second World War (see page 102). The name of its corridors recalls the names of the Ghetto's alleys: Vlasgang (flax alley), Witte Broodgang (white bread alley) and Zwarte ketelgang (black kettle alley).

THE ETS HAIM LIBRARY ⑪

Mr. Visserplein 3, 1011RD Amsterdam
• Visit by appointment by phoning 020 428 25 96

The oldest Hebrew library in the world

The Ets Haim library, called the library of the tree of life, is the oldest still-functioning Jewish library in the world. Today, it has a collection of 30,000 volumes and 500 manuscripts dating from 1484 to the present day, the great majority in Hebrew. They are particularly useful for understanding the history of the Jewish people in the 17th and 18th centuries. The library was founded in 1616, in the heart of the "Academia e Yesiba" seminary, also known as the Ets Haim Talmudic College. The aim of this institution was to provide a secular and religious education to enable Sephardic Jewish immigrants to integrate into the Dutch environment while preserving Jewish tradition. It is an example, ahead of its time, of integration without assimilation. Since 1675, the library has been housed in the range of buildings that surround the Portuguese Synagogue, an imposing monument of the 17th century.

It sits beside the auditorium of the seminary, where the faithful can gather on Sundays during cold winters, since the synagogue is not heated. In 1889 David Montezinos, at that time librarian of this establishment, donated his private collection to the library. Since then, the library has also been called the Livraria Montezinos in his honour. Classified in 2003 in UNESCO's "Recollections of the World" register, the collection gives an idea of the humanistic ideals of the 17th century and of the birth of Sephardic culture in Spain and Portugal. In addition to the theological aspect, the library brings together works on a range of subjects including history, language and literature, but also medicine and economics. The majority of the library's works are available on microfiche through MMF publications.

Each 3rd Thursday evening, except during Jewish religious events, you can listen to a concert at the Portuguese synagogue while enjoying the view of more than a thousand candles. (check the agenda on www.portugesesynagoge.nl)

AMSTERDAM, CENTRE OF INTERNATIONAL PUBLISHING

In the 17th century, Amsterdam was one of the few towns to ensure press freedom and rapidly became an international centre for the publication and sale of books. After the establishment in 1627 of the first Hebrew publisher, Rabbi Menasseh Ben Israel, Amsterdam rapidly became the undisputed centre of Hebrew publishing. Jews from all over the world came to the town to get their work printed and published. To earn their keep during their stay, often lengthy due to the re-working of their books, they worked as invited teachers at Ets Haim. Numerous traces of their lives and their work can be found in the collection's manuscripts.

TO SEE NEARBY

THE SYNAGOGUE OF THE RENEWAL, SYMBOL OF DUTCH TOLERANCE

Beit Ha'Chidush • Nieuwe Uilenburgerstraat 91, 1001LC Amsterdam
• Kabbalat Shabbat, first Friday each month at 8pm
• Check the timetable on the website www.beithachidush.nl/kalender
• Tel.: 020 623 77 91

The shipyards of Uilenburg Island were founded in the 17th century and progressively moved to the Eastern Islands (Oosterlijke eilanden). Subsequently, the Ashkenazy Jews who arrived from Eastern Europe moved into this area and since 1724 there has been a synagogue, here, at No 91. The current synagogue dates from 1766.

At the time of its last renovation, the progressive Beit Ha'Chidush Jewish community took it over. Created in 1995 by Jews with a combination of secular and religious experience, the community strives to be seen as accessible, multicoloured and concerned with the renewal of Judaism. Here one is not concerned about gender or sexual orientation. It is only necessary to have one Jewish parent. Elisa Klapheck, the current Rabbi and first woman Rabbi in The Netherlands, recently wrote that Beit Ha'Chidush has re-oriented the Jewish religion in Europe, starting with Jewish life in The Netherlands, which will lead to a European Jewish identity.

MOKKUM, THE OLD JERUSALEM OF THE WEST

In the Jodenbreestraat and the Sint Antoniesbreestraat, several old 17th-century houses stand amongst modern buildings dating from 1978. This surprising mix is explained by the history of this Jewish area of Amsterdam.

From the 17th century, the great religious tolerance of the town attracted marranos or secret Jews (also known as Anusim) from the Iberian Peninsular who sought to escape persecution. Then, fleeing countries in Eastern Europe, Ashkenazy Jews also found refuge in The Netherlands, thus forming the greatest Jewish community in Europe (120,000 people), hence the title "Jerusalem of the West". Mokkum is the name of Amsterdam in Yiddish. During the Second World War, almost all the residents of this area were deported to Germany and the houses were abandoned. The winter of 1945, which was particularly dire, gave Amsterdammers the idea of pillaging the area to get fuel for their fires: furniture, beams and staircases from these houses were used as heating fuel. Having been occupied by squatters in the 1970s, the area was remodelled under the aegis of the architects Hans Hagenbeek and Aldo van Eyck.

The first project proposed the demolition of numerous houses in the Nieuwmarkt quarter, to make way for a fast highway and a new metro line. It led to intense riots in 1975 and was abandoned in favour of a reconstruction that was more respectful of the urbanism of the past, which enabled numerous buildings to be preserved, such as the Pinto house.

SEA LEVEL AT AMSTERDAM ⓭

The N.A.P. pile
• Amstel 1, 1011NV Amsterdam
Museum at the Bezoekerscentrum
• Open Thursday to Saturday 10am-5pm
• Extended opening hours in the summer
• Entry charge
• Tel.: 020 623 98 86

The proof that Amsterdam really is under water...

Near the Waterlooplein access to the Metro, a big wall panel and tubes measuring different water levels help one understand the extent of the battle between Amsterdam and the sea.

Amsterdam, like the whole western part of The Netherlands, is below sea level and is only protected by the dikes and by dunes. It is not surprising, then, that measuring water levels is undertaken so minutely.

Measuring the level of the tide is related to a reference level, meant to represent normal water level in Amsterdam (in Dutch, Normaal Amsterdams Peil or N.A.P.)

Johannes van Hudde (see page 133), Mayor of Amsterdam, calculated this level in 1683 by reference to the average level of the river IJ in the 17th century. It was adopted as the reference level throughout most of Europe (on the same subject see Unusual and Secret Marseille, in the same series).

Upon entering the passage, one sees three great glass tubes indicating sea levels: in the first tube is measured the level of the North Sea according to the state of the tide (based on the coastal town of IJmuiden) and in the second tube the level in the town of Vlissingen (in Zeeland). At high tide the water nearly comes up to knee level. The third tube is the most worrying as the water is nearly 5m above your head: it's the level reached in Zeeland during the great floods of 1953.

The normal level (N.A.P.) is indicated by a scale on a white pole with a bronze calibration indicator. From Helsinki to Rome, this serves as a point of reference for road construction or sub-marine excavation.

On the wall, a stone panel depicts a cross-section of the ground at different key points in The Netherlands. This representation enables one to take into account the very special geology of the zone. Amsterdam was constructed on wooden piles that rest on the first layer of sand, about 12m below street level. Today, the use of concrete in foundations enables the second layer to be reached, which ensures greater stability and makes possible the construction of much taller buildings. The first metro line, built in 1966, rests on the first bed of sand, while the new line will rest on the second bed, at 24m deep, which accounts for the cost and the difficulties of construction.

The drawing represents the sea at high tide. The level of the water in the canals is adjusted to be 40cm under the N.A.P. To learn more, enjoy the visit of the small museum in the Bezoekerscentrum.

MEMORIAL TO THE JEWISH CHILDREN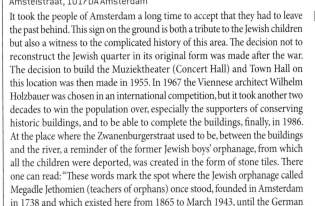
Amstelstraat, 1017DA Amsterdam

It took the people of Amsterdam a long time to accept that they had to leave
the past behind. This sign on the ground is both a tribute to the Jewish children
but also a witness to the complicated history of this area. The decision not to
reconstruct the Jewish quarter in its original form was made after the war.
The decision to build the Muziektheater (Concert Hall) and Town Hall on
this location was then made in 1955. In 1967 the Viennese architect Wilhelm
Holzbauer was chosen in an international competition, but it took another two
decades to win the population over, especially the supporters of conserving
historic buildings, and to be able to complete the buildings, finally, in 1986.
At the place where the Zwanenburgerstraat used to be, between the buildings
and the river, a reminder of the former Jewish boys' orphanage, from which
all the children were deported, was created in the form of stone tiles. There
one can read: "These words mark the spot where the Jewish orphanage called
Megadle Jethomien (teachers of orphans) once stood, founded in Amsterdam
in 1738 and which existed here from 1865 to March 1943, until the German
occupiers burst into the house and deported the children. Three adults volun-
tarily accompanied the 100 children to the extermination camp of Sobibor.
None of them returned. May their memory be blessed."

THE ROLE OF YOUNG ORPHAN BOYS IN THE JEWISH COMMUNITY

Young orphan boys played a particular role in the Jewish community.
They walked before the coffin of a council member at his burial and
recited the Kaddish for members of the council who had no children.
The Kaddish is one of the most important and most frequently uttered
prayers of the Jewish Liturgy. After the death of a father, his sons must
recite the Kaddish for several months. If the deceased had no son,
or his son could not fulfill this task, it could be delegated to orphans.
Since its foundation in 1738 by Ashkenazi Jews, the council of the
Megadle Jethomiem concerned itself with placing orphans with families
who provided their board, lodging and education. As the number of
orphans grew, this approach became more difficult to achieve. At the
end of the 19th century, it was decided to build orphanages. The first
was opened in 1836 and the second in 1865. After the Second World
War, the orphanage served as a departure point for young boys
going to Israel. The building was sold, and then demolished in 1977.

STATUE OF SPINOZA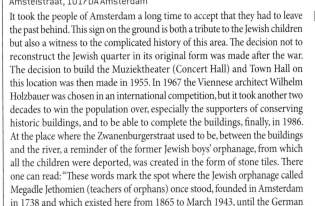
On the Zwanenburgwal, a bronze statue of the philosopher Baruch Spinoza, by
the sculptor Nicolas Dings, was erected on 24 November 2008 at the entrance
of the former Jewish quarter where he grew up. The face is a reproduction
of the one used on the old 1000 florin notes. On his greatcoat, the parrots
symbolize the immigrants and the sparrows the locals. Next to the statue,
lays a cut stone which reminds of his profession, optic lens cutter, and also
illustrates his state of mind: universe as a model, shaped by the human mind.

LOODS ONGNS MEGGAL NEGGRAL FRIES ALBE

AMSTERDAM OPGERICHT

IN 1738 ELDERS IN

VAAR HET

NORTHWEST RING CANALS - JORDAAN

THE "WEST INDIES" HOUSE ❶

Het West-Indisch Huis, Herenmarkt 99, 1013EC Amsterdam
• Tel.: 020 625 75 28 • Conference rooms
managed by the Taste company

> **New York, Brazil, Curacao, Peter Stuyvesant and Prince Maurits**

The "West Indies" House is a symbol of the historic relationship between The Netherlands and the United States of America. This imposing building was built in 1617 and was first used on the ground floor as a slaughterhouse and meat market and on the first floor as a guardroom for the soldiers of the city guard. From 1623 and till 1657, the West Indies Company (W.I.C.) occupied it as its headquarters. They extended the building with two wings around a central courtyard, at the back of the building.

In 1625, the governors of the W.I.C. decided to create a fort in New Amsterdam, on the island of Manhattan. Its first general governor was Peter Stuyvesant. You will notice an attractive bronze statue depicting him above the fountain in the inner court. This fort laid the foundation of New York City. The other key colony was in Brazil. There, the sugar cane plantations were managed by Prince Maurits, thanks to whom we enjoy the Mauritshuis museum in The Hague. We must not forget Curacao in the Dutch Antilles, still part of The Netherlands.

In 1660, the building took the function of "herenlogement" (gentlemen's lodgings). After 1825, it was used as a Lutheran hospice for orphans and old people. On the main façade of the building facing the Haarlemmerstraat, the Lutherans added a swan (see page 111) on the pediment.

After the great fire of 1975, the building was renovated and is now used as a conference centre. It also houses the John Adams Institute, which aims to develop cultural exchanges between The Netherlands and the U.S.A.

TO SEE NEARBY

THE "NEVER AGAIN" GABLE STONE ❷

On the Prinsengracht canal, at No 9, a gable stone reads "Nooit weer" ("Never again"). It dates from 1976 and was donated to the owner of the house by the builder who renovated it, in remembrance of a particularly difficult job.

TO SEE NEARBY

GABLE STONE FROM THE W.I.C. BAYA D TODOS OS SANCTOS ❸
Rozenstraat 144, 1016NZ Amsterdam

In May 1624, Admiral Jacob Willekes, leading the W.I.C. fleet, berthed his ships in the bay of San Salvador on the east coast of Brazil. Though the population resisted, the city was rapidly taken. The inhabitants fled the invaders. The account of this epic venture created a considerable stir in Amsterdam, where the editor Claes Jansz. Visscher quickly published an illustrated book about it. The engraving that illustrated this book was used by the stone carver of the gable stone as an inspiration for his work. It depicts the ships of the W.I.C. fleet entering the bay under the fire of the defending cannons.

THE W.I.C. FOR WEST-INDISCHE COMPAGNIE

This company was founded in 1621 on the same basis as the V.O.C. and had an office in 5 of the main towns in The Netherlands which shared the arming of the expedition ships as follows: Amsterdam 4/9ths, Middelburg 2/9ths, Hoorn, Rotterdam and Groningen 1/9th each.

This limited company was composed of 74 members in total, 19 of whom met every day as a council of administration called "De Heren XIX" (The nineteen gentlemen).

The W.I.C. had the monopoly on the West Indies trade, including the West coast of Africa, America and the Caribbean islands, engaging in triangular trade: shipping cargoes to Africa, transporting slaves to America and returning with cargoes of sugar, tobacco and ores.

Amongst the famous personalities of the W.I.C., Piet Heyn, naval admiral and legendary character, took much booty from the Spanish, especially on the Cuban coast. This piracy came to an end after the Münster treaty, signed in 1648 to acknowledge the reconciliation of the Dutch with the Spanish.

Between Peperstraat and 's Gravenhekje, on the corner of Prins Hendrikkade, you can find the old warehouse of the W.I.C.. Built in 1641, it used to host the organization's meetings after 1657, when it was forced to leave the building on the Herenmarkt, due to financial difficulties.

THE SWAN OF THE LUTHERAN ROUND TEMPLE ❹

Kattengat 1, 1012SZ Amsterdam
• Venue managed by the Renaissance Hotel Amsterdam
• Visit on request by phoning 020 621 22 23

> *"There, where I die, a great bird will rise up"*

The round Lutheran temple is also known as "Koepelkerk" or dome church and was built between 1668 and 1671 for the numerous Germans who had immigrated to The Netherlands to take advantage of the economic prosperity there. On the highest point of this remarkable building, one can spot a swan. It can be seen even better from the Haarlemmerdijk. Adriaan Dortsman, the architect, conceived this temple in a very recognizable formal classical style, with its Doric columns and rectangular windows. The building was crowned by a dome with a little tower, also called a "lantern" as bell towers were exclusive to the Reformed Church. The temple has been restored several times, notably following fires in 1822 and 1993. One shouldn't miss the opportunity to attend a concert in this acoustically exceptional building, and enjoy the well-known organs of Johan Bätz. From afar, above the dome, the remarkable swan marks the location, like a weather vane. In the 15th century, Jan Hus, a theologian of Czech origin, was the first to question the Catholic faith. The name Hus also means Goose. He was condemned to be burned at the stake and his dying words were, "On the place where I die, a great bird will rise up." It is for this reason that a swan is represented on Lutheran temples and houses.

TO SEE NEARBY

THE DECORATIVE PLAQUE SHOWING THE STAGES OF PAPER MAKING ❺
Herengracht 105, 1011RZ Amsterdam

This plaque measures 66x133 cm and dates from 1649. It was produced at the request of Pieter Haack. As a comic strip cartoon would, it shows the way paper was made. At the top centre, a woman is sorting out pieces of cloth: then the story continues below, on the right, where one can see a water wheel, which crushes the fabric and turns it into the pulp from which the paper will be made. At bottom middle, the paper is strained of its moisture. On the left, the paper thus produced is dried in presses between layers of felt. At top right, the sheets of paper are hanging up to dry. Finally, at top left they are being wrapped up ready to be sold.

THE SMALLEST HOUSES OF AMSTERDAM

- Singel 7, 1012VC Amsterdam, 1.01 metre wide, scarcely more than the width of its front door. Its façade is in fact the corner of a much larger building.

- Singel 166, 1015AH Amsterdam, 1.84 metres wide, with 2 floors.

- Oude Hoogstraat 22, 1012ZJ Amsterdam, 2.02 metres wide, about 6 metres deep. It is situated alongside the 17th-century door, designed by the architect Hendrick de Keyser, which gave access to the north aisle of the Walloon Church, whose principal entry is situated on the street round the corner (Oudezijds Achterburgwal), on a little square (Walenpleintje) along a canal. In this tiny house, visitors to the church were given hand warmers.

- Haarlemmerstraat 43, 1013EJ Amsterdam. "De Groene Lantaarne". The smallest restaurant in Amsterdam, by the narrowness of its façade. The building is wider at the back.

- Stromarkt 7, 1012SM Amsterdam, once a little drugstore, today transformed into an office. Access via the neighbouring building.

- Gravenstraat, 1012NL Amsterdam, between Nos 17 and 19. Total surface 3.5m². It is the smallest shop in Amsterdam, also called the nest of the Nieuwe Kerk, as it is built just alongside.

- Molsteeg 5, 1012SM Amsterdam, 4-storey building with a charming bell gable dating from 1644.

- Prinsengracht 4, 1015DV Amsterdam. Small 5-storey house.

- Korsjespoortsteeg 9, 1015AP Amsterdam. Barely over 2 metres wide.

- Prinsengracht 1047, 1017KP Amsterdam. Six floors for this delightful doll's house, only 3 metres wide and 3 metres deep.

WHY ARE THE AMSTERDAM HOUSES SO NARROW ?

In the Golden Age, property taxes were based on the width of the façade of the house. Thus grew the custom of building deep houses with narrow staircases. Moving furniture by the staircase was impossible, so the main roof-beam or hoisting-beam was equipped with a hook, to enable a pulley to be attached for hoisting furniture up to the upper floors and goods to the attic.

In this era of mobile elevators, Dutch furniture movers and builders still prefer to use the pulley – it is quicker and more practical.

TO SEE NEARBY

THE PRISON CELLS OF THE TORENSLUIS ❻
Oude Leliestraat, above the Singel

The bridge or lock of the tower ("Torensluis") is particularly wide, at 39 meters. It is one of the oldest stone arched bridges of Amsterdam. It stands on the location of an old lock from the 17th century; originally, this was the location of one of the towers of the first medieval town ramparts. In 1616, a new tower ("Janroodepoortstoren") was built on the bridge, with a gaol. But it leaned so much that it had to be demolished in 1829. In the absence of funding to rebuild it, its location was recorded on the ground. The prison cells were located in the basement of the bridge, and one can still see the barred windows. Note also the very large bust of the 19th-century socialist writer Multatuli (1820-1887), whose real name was Eduard Douwes Dekker and who lived close by.

MULTATULI MUSEUM ❼
Kosjespoortsteeg 20, 1015AR Amsterdam
• Tel.: 020 638 19 38 • Open every Tuesday from 10am to 5pm,
Saturday and Sunday from 12pm to 5pm

Located in the house where the author was born and lived, the museum exhibits a collection of Multatuli's personal effects (see above and page 178), including his personal library. Multatuli was the writer of the famous book Max Havelaar, translated into 37 languages, which tells the story of a Dutch colonial official who revolts against the oppression of the Javanese people in the Dutch East Indies.

AMSTERDAM, THE TOWN WITH 1700 BRIDGES

Amsterdam is a town made up of 70 islands and a canal network 75 km long.

To ensure the free flow of traffic, pedestrians and boats, much ingenuity has been needed to fit in all the bridges needed. As the town has grown, the number of bridges has never stopped increasing. In the 16th century around 50 bridges were recorded. By the beginning of the 17th century the number had doubled, but by the middle of the same century, with the rapid expansion of the town, the number had grown to 300. Although a number of bridges disappeared when canals were filled in, the 1000th bridge was inaugurated in 1973, over the Westlandgracht to the Rembrandtpark.

Today, Amsterdam has around 1700 bridges. They are an integral part of the architecture of the town. Seventy-two of them, along the inner Singel canal, are classed as historic monuments.

HOW IS THE NUMBERING OF BRIDGES ARRANGED ?

Since the end of the last century, all the bridges have been numbered. The numbering begins with the arched bridge between the Singel and the Amstel, at the junction of four streets - Amstelstraat, Vijzelstraat, Reguliersbreestraat and the Rokin. The numbering continues by following the circle of the canals and continuing outwards. During the renovation of the port area, thirty new bridges were added, whose numbers begin at 2000.

THE LONGEST BRIDGE

At 500 meters long, the Schellingwouderbrug, which links Zeeburgereiland and Schellingwoude, northwest of Amsterdam, is Amsterdam's longest bridge.

BRIDGE (BRUG) OR LOCK (SLUIS) ?

Traditionally bridges made of wood were called 'brug' and those built of stone were called 'sluis', even though all recent bridges are called 'brug'.

Numerous arched stone bridges had to be demolished in the past and replaced by flat ones, because horse-drawn trams could not get over them. Hence the 'Hogesluis' (the high lock) over the Amstel, takes its name from the stone bridge that was there in the 17th century. The present bridge was designed by W. H. Springer in 1883.

TO SEE NEARBY

THE ORGAN OF THE WESTERKERK
Westerkerk, Prinsengracht 281, 1016GW Amsterdam
- Organ concerts free every Friday at 1pm, from April to October.
- Tel.: 020 624 77 66
- Carillon concerts Tuesdays from 12pm till 1pm

The magnificent organ of the West Church or Westerkerk, dates from 1686 and was built by Roelof Barentsz. Duyschot and his son Johannes. Thirty years later, the organ was enlarged by Christiaan Vater. In 1989, it was entirely restored by the organ builder Flentrop: 3000 pipes were replaced and the original shutters repaired. On the shutters can be seen "dancing David and the Ark of the Covenant" and "Solomon and the Queen of Sheba", painted by Gerard de Lairesse.

Apart from the organ, the Westerkerk is equally known for its magnificent carillon. Its principal bell, which sounds the hours, is installed 85 metres up (the tower is the highest in the town) and was cast by Assuerus Koster in 1636. It is also the heaviest in Amsterdam (7509 kg). The half-hour bell is even higher in the tower and weighs 3700 kg. After 1658, the carillon was replaced by a new one, cast by François Hemony. It was entirely restored in 1959 by Boneventura Eijsbouts.

The bells are rung by hand by volunteers. A carillon player plays with his closed fists and uses his little finger to strike a clapper, which is linked to a bell. In the tower are two very old keyboards that were used with the former carillon.

The imperial crown of the Westerkerk contains 870 pearls; the originals were replaced in the 1970s by glass pearls.

THE CARILLON, A DUTCH INVENTION

The carillon is a Dutch invention and was in former times only used to sound the hour. Amsterdam is the town with the most carillons in the world. Nine of them were created by the Hemony brothers. Born in Lorraine, a region well known in the 16th and 17th centuries for its bell founders, François and Pierre Hemony cast their first bell in The Netherlands in 1641. In 1642, they created their first carillon in Zutphen. Such was the quality of their work that the city of Amsterdam invited them to set up business in the town, bringing with them their knowledge, which François did. He cast 20 carillons, of which a number were exported from The Netherlands. The art of the Hemony brothers greatly contributed to making the carillon a recognized musical instrument. In August 2002, in the wreck of a 17th-century boat not far from the Island of Texel, archaeologists discovered a bell cast by François Hemony in 1658 that had never been rung, but which had been entirely preserved from corrosion.

Carillons can also be heard at the Zuidertoren on Thursdays from 12pm till 1pm, at the Munttoren on Fridays from 12pm till 1pm, and at the Oudekerkstoren on Saturdays from 4pm till 5pm.

THE VAN BRIENEN HOFJE ❾

Van Brienenhofje, Prinsengracht 89-133, 1015DN Amsterdam
• Entry to the right of No 133
• A private place, accessible by the public from Monday to Friday
from 6am till 6pm and on Saturday from 6am till 2pm.
Enjoy this quiet place with respect

> *A hofje as a thanks offering to god*

The hofje van Brienen was built in 1804, by Baron van Brienen. The place is as surprising for its fine architecture as for its amusing history.

The baron, who foolishly got himself shut into his strong room one day, losing hope that anyone would come to help him, at that moment implored God to save him, promising that, if his prayer was answered, he would construct a hofje for poor Catholic couples. And it was answered.

So, in 1797, the baron bought the old brewery (the "Star") and asked Abraham van der Hart to build a hofje there. Looking at the building from the street, one can see the star that shines over the clock of the old chapel and one can still clearly see the surrounding wall of the brewery. During major renovation works in 1997, workers discovered evidence of the past in the cellar: barrels containing water from the river Vecht. This water was used in the 18th century as the base for brewing beer.

Hidden behind the façade is a splendid garden. At the end, on the right, the doors screened lavatories in the past. In the middle of the garden, there are two pumps; one pumped well water or "pomp water", for drinking, the other pumped rainwater or "regenwater", for cleaning, etc.

Originally, the lofts above the apartments were used for storing peat, as fuel for heating, and for drying laundry.

The hofje today comprises 26 apartments of around 70m², with all modern comforts: gas since 1863, running water since 1890, electricity since 1917, private lavatories in the 1960s and showers in the 1970s. Until 1951 they were provided free to couples in need.

Today the proprietor is the Housing Association Woningbouwvereniging Het Oosten, but it is still the managers, including descendants of the Baron, who judge the suitability of applicants and decide who is entitled to live in this little paradise.

Willem van Brienen lived in the house at No 176 Herengracht, known as Sundial House or "Zonnewijzer", because of the sundial on its façade. His father had it built in 1781 by the German architect L.F. Druck. He was a Catholic, a rare thing at that time, so the van Brienen hofje was also a Catholic establishment.

THE HOFJE OF THE SUN OR "ZONSHOFJE" ⑩

Prinsengracht 159, 1015DR Amsterdam
• A private place, accessible by the public from Monday to Friday 10 am to 5pm
• Enjoy this quiet place with respect.

A Mennonite Hofje

Push open the door of No 159 Prinsengracht and find a long corridor leading to the hofje of the Sun or "Zonshofje". This Hofje (see page 138) was originally a secret and well-hidden church. Its history illustrates some of the erring ways of the Anabaptist community in The Netherlands.

The Zonshofje takes its name from the Mennonite church in "De kleine Zon" or "The little Sun" which was located here in 1650.

Mennonitism is a protestant Christian movement that developed in the 16th century in Switzerland, then spread to the north of Germany and to Holland through the person of Menno Simons. Like all the Anabaptist movements, the Mennonites were prosecuted. But after the Alteration in 1578, the Reform municipality tolerated all religions in Holland, under reservation that they not be practised too openly (see page 25). The Mennonite community, over two centuries, split up and regrouped several times, as is exemplified by the Zonshofje.

At the time of the first split of the Mennonites in 1663, one of the communities began to meet in an old brewery on the Singel, which had a sun – or "Zon" - on its façade. For this reason, they were called the Zonnists. In 1674, at the time of another split, a small community installed itself in this building leading off the Prinsengracht. In 1752 another, Friesian, branch called the Noah's Ark, linked up with the Zonnists. Traces are to be seen above the lintel of Nos 163-165, in the form of a carved plaque, representing the animals entering the Ark, two by two, under a benevolent sunbeam. This old church was destroyed in 1755 to build an orphanage and a hofje, for old ladies.

Above the plaque one can read the following text: "Love built us this lodging, hope remains our permanent impulse to see the sun on our souls. To withdraw carefully from our times and thus to depart to the Ark of the Saviour."

This hofje was built in a fashion modern for its time: a three-storey building with large windows, which contained 26 lodgings for couples. In 1830, a wing was added, and then, in 1882, the houses at Nos 157 and 173 Prinsengracht were added to the hofje. Since 1960, the Anabaptist ladies have been replaced by young students.

THE SECRET CHURCH OF THE RED HAT ⓫

De Rode Hoed, Keizersgracht 102, 1015CV Amsterdam
• Tel.: 020 638 56 06

An old secret church of the Remonstrants

The secret Church of the Red Hat provides interesting evidence of a secret cult after the Alteration (see page 25). It is the largest and oldest of the secret churches to have been preserved in The Netherlands.

In 1629, a wine merchant (Antoni de Lange) and a doctor (Jan van Hartoghvelt) bought the buildings, in the name of the church of the Remonstrants, to create a place of prayer. Regarded as heretical in 1619, this liberal branch of Calvinism was nevertheless authorized to pray according to its rites, but in secret. So a chapel was built, replacing a workshop here, around 1630. The organ that one can see in the large hall replaced the original organ in 1862. It was built by P. Flaes, an Amsterdam organ builder.

The church remained Protestant until 1957. After being used for various purposes, it was converted in 1990 into a cultural centre, but kept the charming name of Red Hat.

The buildings at Nos 102 and 104 Keizersgracht were built in 1616 to house the workshop of Hans Jansz. Lenaertsz, a hat maker.
On the façade of No 104, an attractive plaque adorned with a small red hat is a reminder of this history.
Some people claim that a certain Claes Hermansz. Roothoet (whose family name means red hat) lived at No 102, leaving his name to the houses.

WHO ARE THE REMONSTRANTS ?
In the 17th century, Jacob Hermansz., professor of theology in the University of Leyden, founded a Protestant movement which fell out with Calvinism on the question of predestination. He signed his works with his latinized name Jacobus Arminius, hence the name of this group "The Arminians". In 1610, the Arminians submitted a "Remonstrance", or formal protest, to the Assembly of the United Provinces, to demand greater tolerance. This provoked a conflict between Remonstrants and Anti-remonstrants. Initially, until 1618, the Arminians were tolerated, but after a synod held at Dordrecht to formalize the points of divergence, and a change of direction in 1619, the Remonstrants went into exile, not returning until 1626. The Canons of Dordrecht are still the denominational canon law of many reformed churches around the world today.

THE HOUSE WITH THE GOLDEN CHAIN

Keizersgracht 268, 1016 EV Amsterdam

A little chain full of symbolism

The façade of No 268 on the Keizersgracht (the Emperor's canal) is decorated with a small gilded chain.

According to one explanation, the mistress of the house, being unable to find her golden chain, accused her chambermaid of theft. Having found the chain soon after and realizing that she had wrongly accused the maid, she attached the chain in front of the house to declare publicly the innocence of her employee.

A second story recounts that a domestic servant, left alone in the house one night, unmasked a thief disguised as an old woman by noticing his half-shaven beard. In a display of bravery, the young woman killed the robber. The master of the house offered a golden chain to this courageous girl to thank her. But she thought the reward too mean. The ill-tempered servant was dismissed and her master fixed the chain above the door to draw everyone's attention to the ingratitude of which he had been victim. The third story, and probably the true one, goes back to 1620. The proprietor of the house, a merchant named Eliseus Harrel, had ordered cloth from Aix-la-Chapelle. Brigands attacked the transport and only one bundle of cloth, encircled by a chain, finally reached its destination. To recall this incident, the proprietor had the chain gilded and used it to decorate the front of his house. In 1999, during renovation work, the house collapsed and had to be rebuilt exactly as it was. The golden chain continues to decorate the façade and to retain its mystery.

TO SEE NEARBY

THE DECORATIVE PLAQUE OF THE BRASS-FOUNDER
Eerste Rozendwarsstraat 13, 1016 PC Amsterdam

The motif of this lovely decorative plaque is a chandelier with a double crown of candles and the wording "de kerk kroon" or "the crown of the church".
This stone marked the house of Jan Engeringh, brass-founder, who worked brass to produce chandeliers for churches. The house dates from 1725 and the plaque was restored in 2000. The double crown of candles was regilded with gold leaf.

Descartes lived from 1629 to 1635 in a house at No 6 of the Westermarkt. The commemorative stone, placed at the initiative of the French Institute of The Netherlands in 1920, displays one of his quotations: "In what other country can one enjoy such complete liberty?" (from his 'Letter to Balzac'). (See also page 173.)

THE SYMBOLS OF THE TRIANGLES
OF THE HOMOMONUMENT

Westermarkt, 1016DH Amsterdam

⑭

"Such an endless desire for friendship"

Constructed at the initiative of a Dutch gay and lesbian group, to inspire and support homosexuals around the world in their struggle against oppression and discrimination, the Homomonument is a creation of Karin Daan dating from 1979.

Despite its monumental scale, it is possible to pass by without noticing it, so successful was the objective of integrating it into its environment. It is constructed as an immense equilateral triangle, each side measuring 36m long. Each point consists of a triangle, with sides 10m long, made of pink granite, linked to the other triangles by a broken line made of pink bricks. The first triangle is low down, on the Keizersgracht and points towards the house of Anne Frank. The second triangle is integrated in the paving of the Westermarkt in front of the church and points towards the war memorial on Dam Square.

Finally, the third triangle rises upward from the Westermarkt Square and points to the COC Centre or "Centre of Culture and Leisure Activities", a cover name for the Dutch organization of gays and lesbians created in 1946.

On the lower triangle, one can read an excerpt from a poem by Jacob Israël de Haan (1881-1924), the first Dutch writer to have affirmed his homosexuality, which speaks of "such an endless desire for friendship."

The symbolic pink triangle worn by homosexuals, just as Jews wore the yellow star, pays homage to the homosexuals persecuted during the Second World War. Fifty thousand were put to death in concentration camps. It is also a vision of the past, the present and of the future of tolerance.

REPLICAS OF STREETLIGHTS WITH CROWNS ⑮

• Originals on the Dam
• Copies on the Westermarkt and Herenmarkt squares, also Falckstraat and on Prinsengracht, at the intersection with Leidsegracht.

Vestiges of gas street lighting

I n The Netherlands, one owes the concept of street lighting to Jan van der Heyden (see page 67), whose invention quickly gained momentum. 1800 street lamps were installed in Amsterdam in the course of the 17th century.

The first street lamp consisted of an oak post 3 metres high, fitted with a four-light copper lantern, about 60cm high. One light could be opened to facilitate cleaning and lighting. Originally, a mixture of beetroot and linseed oil was burned for lighting. In 1780, Jan Pieter Minckelers discovered gas lighting, but it took until 1820 to be able to control this extremely flammable fuel.

The lanterns with crowns, mounted on a cast-iron post, date from 1883. The crown was a replica of the crown of Maximilian of Austria (see page 67). Three original examples are still to be seen on the Dam in front of the Palace. In 1917, when public lighting was electrified, almost all of these lanterns disappeared.

Since 2008, however, the town of Amsterdam has been progressively reinstalling 1,750 streetlights with a crown, along the grand canals and the Amstel. The latest technology of electric lighting is being used to provide a white light with a warm glow, in contrast to the orange lighting currently in use.

OTHER EARLY EXAMPLES OF TOWN LIGHTING

Until the end of the 17th century, anyone who wanted to walk at night in a town had to be content with moonlight: after curfew only holy places and low-dives were lit.

In Paris, it was an Italian abbot, Laudati de Caraffa, who first had the idea of arranging night lighting. He set up a network of "lantern carriers" at certain points, who, for a few coins, accompanied travellers.

The undeniable success of this initiative, in terms of security, interested Louis XIV, who, by an edict of 2 September 1667, initiated the establishment of oil lanterns in Paris and then progressively in the other principal towns of the kingdom. They were replaced from 1766 by oil street lamps, then by gas from 1799, using a technique perfected by Philippe Lebon. In Berlin, Jan van der Heyden's invention was utilised from 1682, with the installation of 1,600 streetlights.

In London, public lighting became established from 1792, thanks to the discoveries of the Scotsman William Murdoch.

THE VAN HUDDE PLAQUE

Eenhoornsluis, Korte Prinsengracht, 1013GN Amsterdam

> *A symbol of Amsterdam's struggle against the water*

Johannes Van Hudde, former mayor of Amsterdam, was the first to show interest in the difficulties Amsterdammers encountered with water, namely the flooding and the foul odours of the canals. In 1683, he focused on the calculation of the NAP (see page 101). He also had marble plates placed on the 8 principal locks of the town so as to follow the level of the water.

A good example is to be found on the Eenhoornsluis lock which separates the Korte Prinsengracht from the River IJ and which shows, by a horizontal line, the level of the dike, 2.76m above the level of the water in the town: "Zee dyks hoogte, zynde negen voet vyf duym boven stadtspeyl" ("Height of the Sea dikes, nine feet six inches above the level of the town"). The white marble plaque is about 50cm wide and is located on the wall, at the bottom of the opening of the black lock gate, on the northeast side.

On the lock is an old cannon which in former times served to protect the town. It is, of course, no longer in use, but strangely no one considered aiming it in its original direction, that is to say pointing outwards and not towards the town.

The lock itself, called the Unicorn ("Eenhoornsluis"), owes its name to a brewery that was situated at No 21 Korte Prinsengracht, where the St Antonia School stands today. High up on the wall, you can still see an illustration of a Unicorn.

CRABS IN AMSTERDAM

The Chinese crab, which appeared in Amsterdam in the 1930's, probably arrived in the hold of a ship arriving from China.

Today, there are more crabs than people in Amsterdam and they can often be seen coming out of the water at night in search of food, as on the Haarlemmerdijk.

Chinese crabs live in freshwater but reproduce in salt water, so the situation in Amsterdam is particularly suitable for them; the locks of the North Sea Canal, which links Amsterdam to the North Sea, are opened regularly, thus letting in salt water.

Canal water in the direction of the river IJ is sweet above and brackish below, which explains the presence of numerous sorts of fish (herring, salmon, whiting or cod).

In the river IJ and in the Amsterdam-Rhine canal, one even finds freshwater clams, which settle on whatever lies at the bottom of the canals, notably old bikes.

TO SEE NEARBY

THE "DE TWEE STOKVISSEN" WAREHOUSE
Brouwersgracht 162, 1013HB Amsterdam

Above the door of this house, a lovely design represents two dried fish, recalling that the warehouse at the corner of Korte Prinsengracht and Brouwersgracht used to be called the Twee Stokvissen (The Two Dried Fish). From the 17th century, this building housed fish merchants, particularly those handling dried cod imported from Norway. From 1821 till 1971, the firm A. Smit & Zoon dealt in dried fish, cod-liver oil and other types of fish oils.

The designs in the windows above the entrance date from the early 17th century. At that time it was common for buildings to open onto a corridor that needed light. Instead of the usual stone plaque (see page 68) telling about the building, a carved wood or wrought iron screen was used in front of the window above the door. This architectural element reached its apogee in the early 18th century.

TO SEE NEARBY

THE PAPABUBBLE SWEET FACTORY AND SHOP
Haarlemmerdijk 70, 1013JE Amsterdam
• Tel.: 020 626 26 62

Papabubble makes wonderful sweets in every colour of the rainbow. In the middle of the shop's premises, visitors can admire the way sugar is boiled, then coloured and shaped, to produce sweets to chew or suck.
Their workshop can easily produce figurines or letters and can make special items to order.

THE HAARLEM DIKE: AGAINST THE SURGES OF THE RIVER IJ

The Haarlemmerdijk (Haarlem Dike) was constructed in 1612. The aim of this dike was to protect Amsterdam from the surges of the river IJ, which, being open to the sea, was much more liable to surges in the 17th century than it is today. The road leading to Haarlem was protected by a gate.
The first Haarlem gate or "Haarlemmerpoort" was built in 1383, on the left of the later Lutheran Chapel and was destroyed in 1506. Subsequently, travellers to Haarlem knew successively three gates, the last built in 1848 on the Haarlemmerplein in a neo-classical style. The function of these gates at that time was no longer defensive; it was for the collecting of tolls. The building was subsequently turned into apartments. The Haarlemmerstraat, a street that forms an extension of the dike, is, for old Amsterdam, a wide road containing a variety of shops. Notable is the one at number 70, specialising in oils. Also to be found here are numerous 17th- and 18th-century houses. At number 2, the lovely neck gable with, at the top, a vine leaf garland and the motto "De wijn 1729 bergh" indicates that a wine merchant was established here. And don't miss, at number 39, in a very different style, the lovely Art Nouveau house.

BOSSCHEHOFJE AND RAEPHOFJE

Palmgracht 28, 1015LD Amsterdam
• Private premises open nearly every day of the week
• Please respect the calm of this place

> *A living witness of two religions under the same roof*

The two adjoining hofjes (almshouses), the Bosschehofje (founded in 1648 by Arent Dirkz. Bosch, a rich grain merchant, and built to house Protestant women of the reformed faith) and the Raephofje, are little havens of peace right in the heart of Amsterdam. The one Protestant and the other Menonnite, they are a living testimony to the co-existence of the religions in the country.

To enter these hofjes, one should use the entrance door on the Palmgracht. It is more interesting to start by going through the Raephofje, by the door on the right, and then to cross the courtyard that gives you access to the Bosschehofje.

The large interior courtyard was divided for nearly 300 years by a wall and then by a hedge. The evolution of this separation reflects the recent evolution towards more tolerance within the Reformed Church. Crossing the courtyard, at the end one finds a road towards the Bosschehof, on the side of the Palmgracht.

After the war, these small dwellings became insalubrious: they were renovated in 1952-1953. Today, four ladies still live in two apartments upstairs and two apartments downstairs. The windows, with their small panes and window frames from the 18th century, have been preserved. There are more than 110 panes in all.

Leaving the Raephofje, note the stone with a turnip ("*raep*") and the initials and arms of Pietersz. Raep, the Hofje's benefactor. Under the house numbers is an "L" for "*Lidmaat*." This told orphans collecting donations where to ring.

On the Dam Square, on the side of the Krasnapolsky Hotel, is a small and very pretty 18th-century building, recognisable by its lovely Renaissance gable. Looking above the loft window, one can see a carved stone representing a swede or "raep". This house was originally called "'s Hertogenbosch" from the name of the town from which its first owner probably hailed, and from whom Pieter Adriaensz. Raep bought it. The prime location of this house, with a rentable value of 200 florins per year, was sufficient to fund the running costs of the Raepenhofje.

WHAT IS A HOFJE ?

A Hofje (Almshouse) typically comprises an enclosed courtyard surrounded by a group of buildings, often constructed in a U, with an internal garden and a door for observing arrivals and departures. Hofjes were privately funded institutions, something between a convent and a hospice, which developed strongly from the 17th century onwards in the north of Europe.

They are particularly numerous in The Netherlands, providing for single women for whom widowhood equated poverty. But there are exceptions, like that of Mr. Deutz, who created a hofje for his retired employees.

In the Dutch Republican system, the church did not play a great role; rich families took responsibility for caring for the poor. Thus they would have a hofje constructed as a caring act of charity, which was also a means of ensuring that their name passed down positively to posterity.

The motivation to offer a hofje was all the greater when a couple had no child or did not get on with their daughter-in-law. The family would then nominate a male or female cousin as Regent. In Amsterdam many regents are still direct descendants of the benefactors.

In principle, the benefactor of a Hofje also shouldered the upkeep. He might also, for example, make a donation at Christmas or on the occasion of his birthday, in the form of peat for heating or of cheese. The hofje was also frequently attached to the religious community of the donor. After the Alteration of 1578, the Catholic and Anabaptist religions were tolerated as long as their practice was not visible from the outside, which explains why chapels were often constructed in the middle of hofjes.

To live in a hofje meant subjecting oneself to numerous rules. The regents imposed an irreproachable code of conduct, particularly in relation to going to church, not drinking and asking the occupants to pray for them.

At a female hofje, it was even forbidden for the women to receive males over the age of 5 years, even a brother, without leaving the door open.

In exchange for accepting these strict rules, the inhabitants enjoyed free lodging and often received financial aid towards their needs or gifts in kind.

Due to lack of financial means, the majority of hofjes have now been taken over by religious organisations. The regents are still present and maintain their efforts to keep up the continuity of operation.

Over the last 25 years, numerous hofjes have been restored and modernised to introduce the level of comfort and hygiene appropriate to modern life. The doors of hofjes are open during the day. Push them open to admire the beauty within, while respecting the tranquillity of the place.

DISTILLEERDERIJ
A·Y·W
"DeOoievaar"

'THE STORK' DISTILLERY

20

De Ooievaar, Driehoekstraat 10, 1015GL Amsterdam
• Organisation of a tasting on request
• Tel.: 020 626 77 52

*Enjoy
a private tasting
on request*

The distillery of The Stork ("De Ooievaar"), a branch of the van Wees firm of The Hague, was founded in 1883 in the Jordaan to distil genever, liqueur, and eau-de-vie. It is possible to organise tastings there on request.

The Dutch were the first to produce excellent distilled drinks from agricultural products. In the 17th century, the Dutch distillations, based on cognac, cointreau, gin and even rum (see page 47), were known throughout the world. These drinks were exported to numerous countries in the world, which proved to be a very profitable business, hence the importance of the companies which produced them.

Upon entering Driehoekstraat by way of the Palmgracht, one first comes to the distillery, where the copper boiling kettles are visible from the street. Liqueurs are still distilled here, both innovative ones and the more classic ones like genever, always greatly appreciated by the Dutch. The stock is warehoused in this building and totals 80,000 litres. A little further on, on the left on the corner of Palmgracht, is the café where you can enjoy a tasting, choosing between 16 varieties of genever and 60 other liqueurs. Their names, even if no longer popular, recall the past: "the boys of the fields", "the girls of the fields", "forget me not", "absolute happiness", and "the tears of the bride".

The van Wees company has its own tasting venue at No 319 Herengracht (open from Monday to Saturday, from 4:30pm to midnight).

WHY THE STORK ?

Dutch business having always been international, it was easier to have one's brand recognized by a design than by a text which was difficult to translate into all the languages of the world. The choice of an animal design made the brand easier to remember.

Having originated in The Hague, the firm chose the Stork, as this bird is in the arms of the town.

Two gable stones in the Driehoekstraat indicate that genever was distilled there in earlier times: at No 10 one can see a barrel and a barrel-maker's tool, and on the gable stone at No14 a distillery is represented.

THE KARTHUIZER (CARTHUSIAN) HOFJE ㉑

Karthuizerhof, Karthuizersstraat 21-131, 1015LL Amsterdam
• Entrance at the level of No 89

The biggest hofje in Amsterdam

The Karthuizer Hofje (Hojfe of the Carthusians) today has nothing in common with the earlier convent of the Carthusians. The latter was founded in 1394, outside the medieval town where Goudsbloemstraat is located nowadays. Pillaged and destroyed in 1572, it was abandoned and fell into ruins.

On entering the hofje, the largest in Amsterdam, note the names of the families Keizerrijk, Boogert, Peereboom, Vijfvliegen, Opmeer and Vegters over the entrance. In olden days, hofjes were effectively financed by one family or by the organisation called "Huiszittenmeisters", which operated a form of public municipal assistance and was financed by private donations.

The construction of the Karthuizer Hofje was decided upon following the sale of a number of houses received as donations by the organisation, which rendered homage to the donors by inscribing their names on the building.

Above the two doors of the hofje, on the right, one can see the three crosses of St Andrew (the arms of the town of Amsterdam, see page 17) symbolizing the involvement of the town. Straight above, a gable stone represents a ship with two men and a dog (see following page).

The town architect Daniel Staelpert was given the commission for the hofje. In 1651, the doors of the "Huiszitten-weduwehof" (house for widows) opened to accept 110 women, some of whom were admitted with their children.

The hofje was constructed around two gardens used for bleaching the washing, with two large pumps. The water runs through two large taps in the form of dolphins, often used to symbolise living waters. In the corners of the hofje, doors conceal the former "secrets", a Dutch synonym for toilets. The space inside was so small that the doors had central hinges to enable one to enter.

On leaving the hofje, one can see the clotheslines going back to the date of construction.

In the 1970s, the situation having become precarious, these lodgings ceased to house only old people and were opened to a wide variety of tenants. It was only in 1986 that the Woningbedrijf Amsterdam (a public housing body) restored the hofje. The peat lofts were converted into dwellings, creating apartments with two or three rooms.

Opposite the Karthuizerhof is a large playground that occupies the site of the convent's former cemetery.

THE GABLE STONE DEPICTING THE SHIP ❷❷
WITH TWO MEN AND A DOG

Karthuizerhof
- Karthuizersstraat 21-131, 1015LL Amsterdam
- Entrance at the level of No 89

History of the town seal

L egend says that around 1150, during a storm on the Zuiderzee, two men found themselves adrift in a boat with a dog. In his distress, one of the men made an oath that if he was saved he would found a town on the spot to which his dog led him. That's how they found themselves at the mouth of the Amstel, where they built a dam. The foundations of the town of Amsterdam were thus laid.

A century later in 1275, Guy van Henegouwen, Bishop of Utrecht, gave Amsterdam its status as a town. The seal he chose depicted a Medieval boat, which also existed in the arms of the ports of Harderwijk, Stavoren, and Medemblik. At the top of the mast one can see a lion, the arms of the Henegouwen family, an indication that the town of Amsterdam was developed on the family's land. In the boat on the gable stone, two men stand: one carries a flag with the arms of Amsterdam and the three crosses of St Andrew, and the other carries a sword and a shield with the arms of the Henegouwen family, with four lions. Between them is the dog.

A 90-YEAR ERROR
In 1637, the poet Vondel wrote the play called Gijsbrecht van Amstel (Gilbert of Amstel), which was very successful, ensuring it an annual performance on the 1st of January in the municipal theatre for several centuries. He dated it to 1304, and situated it for the most part in the Karthuizer convent. Vondel, however, was clearly ill-informed, as the convent wasn't actually founded until 1394!

TO SEE NEARBY

THE GABLE STONE OF THE WORLD UPSIDE-DOWN ❷❸
At No 53 Lindengracht, you can see an amusing gable stone dating from 1972 where everything is topsy-turvy. The fish are in the tree, the inscription is written from right to left, and the date is upside down. This stone actually commemorates the fact that, until 1895, Lindengracht was a canal.

THE BOUNDARIES OF THE FORMER CEMETERY OF THE NORTH CHURCH ❷❹
Noordermarkt 48, 1015NA Amsterdam

In front of the North Church (Noorderkerk), an area of the pavement is marked out and delineates the playground for neighbourhood children. In fact, the lines denote the boundaries of the old cemetery of the church.

The cemeteries have all disappeared from the centre of Amsterdam. Due to a shortage of space, all the ornaments have been removed from the tombs.
Here, the space has been reused as a public place.

PIANOLA MUSEUM   ❷❺

Westerstraat 106, 1015MN Amsterdam
• Open on Sunday 2pm-5pm, other days by appointment
by phoning 020 627 96 24 • Entry charge
• Theme concerts in the evening,
program available on www.pianola.nl

> *Every hole represents a note, and its diameter the intensity of the playing*

The pianola, or reproducing piano, is a very fine musical instrument whose history began in the United States in 1894. This mechanical piano, which allows pieces recorded on rolls of perforated paper to be played automatically, was extremely successful there. During the gramophone's very early days, nearly 2 million mechanical pianos were built. The economic crisis of the 1930s, though, and the arrival of the radio, were the reasons for this instrument's decline in popularity.

Twenty pianolas can be found in the museum, using a variety of systems, from the mechanism placed above the keyboard of a conventional piano to the system integrated into a superb grand piano.

However, the surprise is probably not in the instruments themselves but in the music they are capable of producing. The name "reproducing piano" is no misnomer and the reproduction of the playing of a pianist is extremely subtle and striking.

To allow the music to be produced with precision, the mechanism of the pianola is based on a pneumatic system. Each location of holes in the paper roll represents a note and the diameter of the hole the intensity. Towards 1910, the system of 88 notes, the equivalent of the 88 notes of the classical piano, became standard around the world.

Even if the majority of rolls are of this type, on a pianola one can only play the rolls produced by the maker of that particular instrument, meaning that there are at least a dozen different types of rolls. The archives of this museum contain about 20,000 music rolls altogether. The musical repertoire is very varied: popular or classical music, opera, operetta… everything that can be played on a piano was put on a perforated roll.

Certain composers even wrote pieces especially for a pianola, pieces which couldn't actually physically or technically be played by hand, even by the most virtuosi of pianists.

The music rolls are preserved in the ancient cellars of this building constructed as a police station in 1905.

In English, the American piano-bar piano is called "Honky Tonk piano", in reference to the Tonk brothers, producers of pianolas in New York at the beginning of the 20th century ("Honky" is an American term for designating Whites, but the word "Honky Tonk" more often refers to a particular type of country music).

THE G. PERLEE BARREL ORGAN MUSEUM ㉖

Westerstraat 119, 1015LZ Amsterdam
• Tel.: 020 624 93 10
• Visit on request

*Witness
of a past age*

Hidden in a vast warehouse in the Jordaan, the workshop of the Gijs Perlee family - which goes back five generations- manufactures, maintains and restores barrel organs. The family business was started in 1932 by Leon Warnies and Gijs Perlee, under the name "Perlee". Descendants of both families still work there, even continuing to compose music and creating new perforated paper cards. They are the last people to maintain this skill in The Netherlands and their instruments find their way around the world.

Unlike a classic organ, the barrel organ is an instrument that produces the music automatically. Originally, as with small music boxes, the organ player moved a large wheel to turn the cylinder. In 1892, perforated cards appeared which folded in harmonica fashion. Easier to stock, they also enabled longer pieces of music to be played.

Music for barrel organs reached its apogee in the 1920s, with composers like the Dutch Piet Maas and the German Carl Frei. With the crises of the 1930s, orders diminished and, after the war, only Gijs Perlee & Son continued to compose new scores for barrel organs.

Although the barrel organ originated in Italy, The Netherlands developed a long tradition around this instrument. In the 1920s, around 30 organs were wheeled through the streets of Amsterdam and played popular melodies and operettas, inviting people to dance. On the front of the organ, marionettes worked automatically, playing a drum or a cymbal rhythmically, to the great fascination of children. To thank him for his music, people threw the organist a few coins, carefully wrapped in paper if tossed from upper stories of buildings.

After the liberation, the development of the gramophone and the radio, which enabled everyone to have music at home, as well as the arrival of the American juke-box brought an end to the career of the barrel organ in public places.

It is possible to rent a barrel organ by the day, with an organist.

THE DIFFERENCE BETWEEN THE BARREL ORGAN AND THE PIANOLA
The barrel organ is a large box with a handle and a slot to insert the perforated paper.
The pianola is a true piano with a small space to insert the perforated paper - like a piano where the artist is invisible.

ANSLO OR CLAES CLAESZ. HOFJE

- First entry: on the right after the Claes Claesz. tavern, Egelantiersstraat 26, 1015PM Amsterdam
- Second entrance: Eerste E1015RW Amsterdam
- Establishment generally private
- Please respect the calm of this place

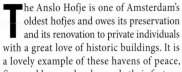

Two names for two eras

The Anslo Hofje is one of Amsterdam's oldest hofjes and owes its preservation and its renovation to private individuals with a great love of historic buildings. It is a lovely example of these havens of peace, financed by people who made their fortunes in the 17th century, and one that has succeeded in surviving through the centuries.

On entering by the door to the right of the restaurant, you arrive in what was the original Anslo Hofje. Note above the entry door the gable stone representing the arms of the family and the inscription "Anslo's Hofje".

In 1615, the rich Anabaptist draper Claes Claesz. and his wife Geert Jans decided to construct a hofje. It comprised three houses behind a little garden and accommodated old people free of charge.

On the right is the old "Zwaardvegershofje" or Hofje of the military outfitters, linked to the sword makers who worked in this quarter. There used to be an entry on Tuinstraat but it no longer exists.

The two hofjes together have taken the name Claes Claesz., from the name of the association which undertook the renovation of the buildings in the early 1970s. This enabled the creation of 60 lodgings for Conservatory and Fine arts students.

In the Anslo Hofje, one can also see, on the right, two doors which led to the toilets. In the middle, above the pretty fountain, is a lion's head upon which is a panel giving thanks to Madurodam.

During the renovation in May 1968, the architect G. Prins discovered that there were box beds in the bedroom. He chose to preserve them, but had them lengthened, as they were originally only 1.6m long.

TO SEE NEARBY

GABLE STONE OF THE "HAND THAT IS WRITING" 28

At No 52 Egelantierstraat, note the lovely gable stone known as "The hand that is writing".
It refers to the schoolmaster Hendrick Wient who lived here in the 17th century and also held the position of public writer.

THE ST ANDREW HOFJE OR "ST ANDRIES HOFJE" ㉙

Egelantiersgracht 137-145, 1015RG Amsterdam
• Private place, open to the public from Monday to Saturday, 9am to 6pm
• Enjoy this quiet place with respect

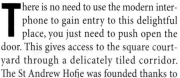

T here is no need to use the modern interphone to gain entry to this delightful place, you just need to push open the door. This gives access to the square courtyard through a delicately tiled corridor. The St Andrew Hofje was founded thanks to

> *The second oldest Hofje in Amsterdam after the Begijnhof*

the legacy of a rich cattle dealer and Catholic bachelor named Jeff Gerritsen. In 1614, his executor and nephew Jan Jacobsz. Oly bought a large piece of land on the Egelantiersgracht on which to build a hofje. It was finished in 1617, making it one of the oldest in Amsterdam. It was called St Andrew after the name of the house were Jan Oly lived. Since 1699, the St Andrew Hofje has been run by the Begijnhof, fulfilling the wish of the last descendent of the family, Anna de Majistratis, who ended her days in the Begijnhof and stipulated that, on her death, the Hofje would be taken over by that institution.

The Hofje has changed greatly through the last three centuries. The entrance was remodelled at the beginning of the 20th century, using pretty tiles. In the 1970s, extensive renovations enabled the transformation of the 36 small lodgings into 22 modern comfortable ones, still assigned to single women between the ages of 30 and 70. Not all traces of the past have been erased. You can see on the right the surprising shape of the doors, which enabled observation of the settlement of the building over the centuries.

TO SEE NEARBY

THE GABLE STONE OF THE "SAVIOUR" ㉚

Inside the St Andrew Hofje, on the left, an attractive gable stone that once marked the entrance to the almshouse represents Christ the Redeemer.
The Hofje was built after the Alteration. The gable stone does not represent St Andrew, as the Saints were not worshiped under Protestant beliefs.

The Chapel, however, built in 1623 within the Hofje, allowed Catholic women to practice their religion in secret. This gable stone was inspired by an etching by Karel van Mander, who produced a series of 14 etchings on religious subjects in 1592. In 1604, he also wrote a book on the theory of painting, which brought him great fame. There is also an attractive example of a gable stone with the theme of Christ the Redeemer in the Begijnhof, to the left of the wooden house.

VREDE·SY·MET·V

THE LEGEND OF THE HOUSE WITH THE HEADS

This double house at No. 13 Keizersgracht, built in 1622 in the purest Dutch Renaissance style, was a project of Hendrick de Keyser's. It is known by the name "the House of the Heads" because of the six heads of the gods of the pantheon that appear on the façade.

Close to the entrance, one can recognize Phoebus, the God of Beauty, with a crown of laurels on his head. Ceres, Goddess of Fertility, is adorned with ears of ripe wheat.

Mars, God of War, is recognisable by his helmet. Minerva, Goddess of Wisdom, stands alongside Bacchus, with grapes and a vine.

Finally, Diana, Goddess of the Hunt, is recognizable by the half-moon in her hair, symbolizing that, according to legend, she hunted at night.

The legend is that the housemaid, left alone in the house one night, went to the outhouse at the bottom of the garden. Seeing a saw moving in a hole in the fence, she armed herself with an axe and decapitated six burglars, one after the other.

In 1922, a commemorative plaque was placed with an inscription in Czech, reading "Here lived J.A. Komensky (1656-1670)".

The proprietor at that time, Laurens de Geer, welcomed into his home, until the end of his life, the famous Czech philosopher, grammarian and pedagogue Jan Amos Komensky, known as Comenius.

THE HERMETIC PHILOSOPHY LIBRARY

Bloemstraat 15, 1016KC Amsterdam
• Tel.: 020 625 80 79
• Open Monday to Friday 9:30am till 12:30pm and 1:30pm till 5pm
• Entry charge

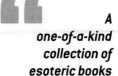

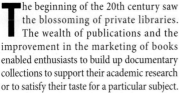

A one-of-a-kind collection of esoteric books

The beginning of the 20th century saw the blossoming of private libraries. The wealth of publications and the improvement in the marketing of books enabled enthusiasts to build up documentary collections to support their academic research or to satisfy their taste for a particular subject.

Born in 1941, Joseph R. Ritman built his fortune on the sale of plastic cutlery, starting with the market for meals served on airliners. This did not, however, prevent him from developing a great interest in spirituality.

It seems that he started collecting books when he was very young, after his mother gave him a copy of the 17th-century book "Aurora" by Jacob Böhme.

His library is world-renowned. It contains 20,000 books and manuscripts specialising in Christian hermetic philosophy, more than a hundred manuscripts dating from before 1550, and about 5000 books dating from before 1800.

In 1984, Mr. Ritman decided to turn his collection into a public one, but as a result of his expenditure on books and in the world of arts, he ran into financial difficulties. Even though his collection was considered to be part of the national heritage, a part of it was sold at auction in London by ING bank. Mr. Ritman sold his company, enabling him to buy them back.

In 2007, the Dutch State bought a third of his collection for 19 million euros. His merit in the world of literature has been rewarded with several prizes, including the silver medal of the Royal Academy of Arts and Sciences (KNAW) in 2002.

The presence of Mr. Ritman's collection is one of the reasons for the creation of a chair of hermetic philosophy at the University of Amsterdam.

THE GABLE STONES OF THE BURGLAR

Elandsgracht 73, 1016TV, Amsterdam

Where is Sjako's treasure hidden?

On 15 October 1999, two gable stones were inaugurated on the building at No 73 Elandsgracht, in memory of the Amsterdam bandit, thief and housebreaker Jacob Frederik Muller. Muller, of German origin, who lived in the 18th century, was known as "Sjako" or "Jaco".

In 1714, at the age of 25, he fell into the hands of the law and was condemned to 25 years imprisonment. To prevent him from escaping, he was made to wear a sort of wooden manacle in which his left hand was imprisoned. Even so, he managed to escape and took refuge in the old warehouses on Elandsgracht, which became known as "Sjako's Fort". He was once again arrested and beheaded on the Nieuwmarkt Square in 1718.

The first gable stone depicts the 'fort' and the second Sjako himself, the designs having been inspired by a painting in the Amsterdam Museum, even though it can't be proved that Sjako actually lived at this location. Sjako was a character rather liked by the Dutch; a bit like Robin Hood he took from the rich to give to the poor. Numerous Dutch writers have picked up on this legend.

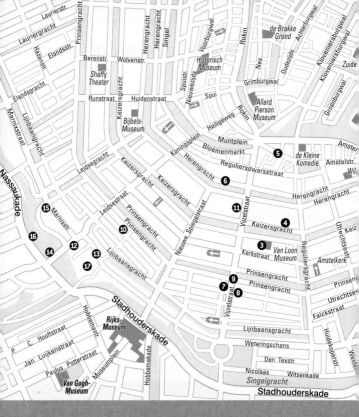

SOUTHEAST RING

CANALS - PLANTAGE

THE 'BLOOD-STAINED' HOUSE

Amstel 216, 1017AJ Amsterdam

> *Mysterious 17th-century graffiti*

The double house at No 216 Amstel is typical of the last period of Dutch Classicism. Built in 1670 by Adriaan Dortsman - the date can be seen in Roman numerals above the front door - the house is however unique; the façade forms an exact square and each level has three windows, in contrast with the normal two-by-two symmetry in double houses. At one time, there were glazed access doors leading to the service entrances on either side of the entrance. These have been converted to windows.

Around 1750, the house was embellished with ornaments typical of a French baroque influence. Today, this majestic house has been modified, with a "penthouse" on the roof terrace, which, however, is not visible from the front.

In 1675, Coenraad van Beuningen moved into the house. This important person, elected mayor six times and appointed ambassador to various European countries, married Jacoba Bartolotti van den Heuvel in 1686. This marriage, to a woman 18 years younger than him, was not a happy one. During the later years of his life, his melancholy gradually turned into madness. It is said that this madness led van Beuningen to paint astonishing red symbols on the façade of his house: Hebraic letters, a pentagram, octagons, three-masted ships, flags, as well as his own name and that of his wife (van Beuningen and Jacoba).

The story is that van Beuningen created this graffiti with his own blood, hence the name of the house: "blood-stained".

TO SEE NEARBY

THE SIX HOUSE

Amstel 218, 1017AJ Amsterdam
• Visit by appointment by phoning 020 622 44 10 • Entry charge

This house has belonged to the Six family since 1915. Their ancestor, a famous mayor of Amsterdam originally from Lille, commissioned Rembrandt to paint his portrait in 1654. Thanks to the Six Foundation, both the house and this famous painting have been preserved.

TO SEE NEARBY

THE BALUSTRADE OF THE STAIRCASE OF THE VAN LOON HOUSE **❸**
van Loon museum, Keizersgracht 672, 1017ET Amsterdam
• Tel.: 020 624 52 55 • Entry charge
• Open from Friday to Monday from 11am to 5pm

Built in the Golden Age and renovated in the 18th century by Abraham van Hagen and his wife, this patrician residence bears the names of its early owners, wrought into the banisters.

In 1671, a rich Flemish merchant, Jeremias van Raey, commissioned Adriaan Dortsman to build two houses. Above the first one, at No 672, are two statues of Vulcan and Ceres, while Minerva and Mars are represented above the second, at No 674. Mr. van Raey inhabited the second house and rented the first one to the famous painter Ferdinand Bol, one of Rembrandt's pupils, who lived there with a rich widow. It was she, or rather her fortune, that encouraged Ferdinand Bol to give up painting.

In 1752, the house was bought by Dr. van Hagen, husband of Catharina Trip (see also page 29). They carried out an extremely detailed renovation in the spirit of the 18th century. For instance, in the painted room on the first floor, one can wonder at the perfect symmetry of the room, with one door disguised in the panelling while another - false - door was added opposite the fireplace. The most surprising feature, though, is certainly the owners' names formed in the copper banisters of the monumental stair-case, installed at this time. Hendrik van Loon bought the house in 1884. At the beginning of the 19th century, the van Loon family was ennobled; their arms are visible on the pediment. They are composed of three heraldic symbols deriving from a main structural element of the windmills, which, in the Middle Ages, were in the family's possession in Loon op Zand. Above them are two black heads, with their faces turned, wearing silver headbands and gold earrings, a reference to the role the family played in the V.O.C. The house is still inhabited by the widow of the last van Loon descendant, Jonkheer Mauritz van Loon. It took 30 years to complete the last renovation piece: the addition of beautiful painted wallpapers from Jurriaen Andriessen in the reception rooms. Those wallpapers, typical from the interior decoration from the 18th Century (see page 165), were originally in the castle Drakensteyn, in the area of Baaren. The coach house in the back of the garden has recently been renovated, in the style from the 17th Century.

THE ANCIENT HOUSE NUMBERING SYSTEM IN AMSTERDAM

Above doors, you can read, for example, D7 G15 No 712. These numbers indicate: 15th locality, of the 7th district, house No 712. They are remnants of the first house numbering system dating from 1796, devised by Professor J.H. van Swinden. A number like AA22 is from a later date and indicated a neighbourhood number.

With the arrival in 1806 of the first King of Holland, Louis Bonaparte, Napoleon's brother, who reigned until 1810, Amsterdam houses were numbered starting from the current Central Station.

As in all the countries where Napoleon left this inheritance, the uneven numbers start on the left.

THE GARDEN OF THE GEELVINCK HINLOPEN HOUSE MUSEUM ❹

Musée Geelvinck Hinlopen huis • Herengracht 518, 1017HL Amsterdam
• Entry at Keizersgracht 633 • Tel.: 020 639 07 47
• Open on Wednesday to Monday, from 11am till 5pm
• Concert on Sunday at 4:45pm • Entry charge

> *One of the largwest gardens of the canal district*

This lovely house, restored with great care, is worth a visit not only for its interior but also for its very beautiful garden, one of the largest in the canal area. Albert Geelvinck bought a parcel of land on the Herengracht in 1683, where he built a double house, starting in 1687.

The interior consisted of a central corridor serving a salon or great room on the right and an office on the left. As with many houses on the canals, the original plot was 50 metres deep. Several years later Mr. Geelvinck purchased the building at the end of his garden, whose frontage was on the Keizersgracht. It had an enormous garden of about 1000m², about four times the average of most houses, with an outbuilding, where the entrance to the museum is now situated.

One can enjoy the arrangement of the garden created here by the landscape gardener Robert Broekema. Around a pond in the form of a cross, nature has been tamed in the style of a French garden, and yet it also exudes an abundance reminiscent of an English cottage garden. At the reception level of the house, on the main floor, there are four very well-preserved rooms.

In the red room, note the very fine ceiling in the style of Louis XV. In the blue room, the walls are covered with paintings undertaken by Egbert van Drielst in 1788. The paintings represent country scenes: a hunter with his dogs, a merchant and his donkey, a fisherman, a shepherd strolling, and a couple of lovers on the grass. The library has a neo-classical ceiling, whose style was inspired by that of the Roman Emperor Diocletian's palace in Split, Croatia.

PAINTED WALLPAPERS

Painted wallpapers (beschilderde behangsels) are a classic element of 18th-century interior decoration. Although they look like wallpaper, they are actually painted on large pieces of canvas. Aligned precisely within the wainscoting, and often installed in reception rooms, they represent country scenes, with the horizon line placed at eye-level. Generally, three decorated panels form a story. The fourth panel is that of the windows, opening on to the garden, a little like a large trompe-l'œil, or deceptive picture, giving the impression of a voyage. The majority of houses that still have such decorative paintings are not open to the public; the Council Room of the Bazel building (see page 179), the van Loon house (see previous page), the Geelvinck Hinlopen museum and the Grachten huis (Herengracht 386) are exceptions. Nevertheless there are some dwellings with painted wallpaper in the rooms beside the street, and you may thus be able to see them in passing, if they are not protected from the sun by shutters or curtains: Herengracht 40 (J. Andriessen) Keizersgracht 240 Keizersgracht 269 (W. Uppink), Keizersgracht 319 (van Elders).

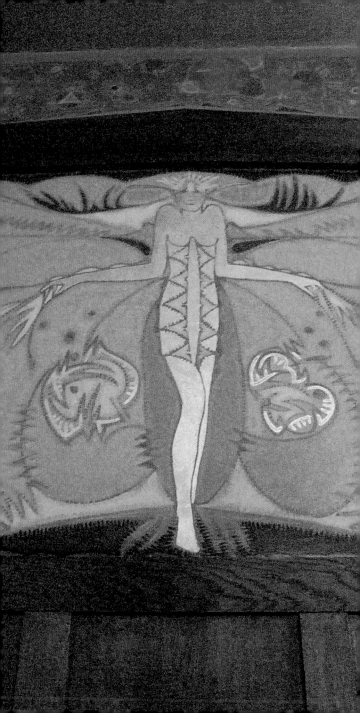

THE LADIES OF PIETER DEN BESTEN ❺

Pathé Tuschinski
Reguliersbreestraat 26-34, 1017CN Amsterdam
• Tel.: 0900-1458
• Open Monday to Sunday from 11:30pm till the last performance
• Accessible if you go to watch a film in the main hall (no1), on the second balcony • Guided visit for individuals once a month • Entry charge
• http://www.pathe.nl

> **Art Deco beauties restored to their original elegance**

A masterpiece of architecture and of decoration, the Theatre-Cinema Tuschinski possesses, behind the entry hall, superb frescos, which decorate the corridor and even the upper circle. They bear witness to the desire of Abraham Icek Tuschinski to make his theatre continually more lovely and impressive.

Mr. Tuschinski did not actually intend to settle in The Netherlands. He had left his native Poland in order to embark at Rotterdam and emigrate to the United States. He was so attracted by the town, though, that he stayed and built his fortune in the new business of cinema halls. Spurred on by the success of his first four cinemas in Rotterdam, this man, with his remarkable sense of business, wanted to attract the public of the Capital by creating a sumptuous building as a monument to cinema. On 28 October 1921, this astonishing building, with its mixture of Art Deco and Amsterdam School influences, was opened.

In the course of renovation work in 2000, the superb frescos of Pieter den Besten were discovered, hidden under several coats of paint dating, in particular, from the time of the German occupation during the Second World War. When the theatre was built in 1918-21, Pieter den Besten, an artist of the Rotterdam School, painted the frescos of women, known as 'the butterfly ladies', that you can see in the orchestra stalls of the main hall.

It is thought that, in celebration of the theatre's 10th anniversary, Abraham Tuschinski, pleased with the previous work of Pieter den Besten, commissioned him to produce splendid new frescos to decorate the walls of the upper circle. They consisted of 18 stylized ladies, superb illustrations of Art Deco style.

In the foyer, high up on the wall, between the two ticket offices, there is a small window. It belongs to the former office of Abraham Tuschinski. Totally committed to his role of director, he liked to keep an eye on the level of attendance in the theatre.

LOVE SEATS FOR ROMANTIC COUPLES
For romantic couples, the Tuschinski cinema created "love seats", a wide seat for two with a table where champagne is served: 19.50 euros per person, glass of champagne included.

THE CATS COLLECTION ❻

Kattenkabinet, Herengracht 497, 1017BT Amsterdam
- Open Mon-Fri 10am - 4pm, Sat and Sun 12noon -5pm
- Entry charge
- Tel.: 020 626 67 64

> *Cats in paintings by Picasso, Rembrandt, Toulouse-Lautrec...*

I n this district, where most of the fine houses have been taken over by lawyers and banks for their offices, this surprising little museum, dedicated to our feline friends, shows innumerable works of art representing cats.

The Cats Collection is situated in a lovely house, built in 1667 like its neighbouring twin, by the brothers Willem and Adriaan van Loon (see also page 162). The house remained in the family until 1725. It was subsequently renovated in 1837, and, as with many houses along the canals, the main entrance was lowered to street level. Purchased in 1885 by the banker Pieter van Eeghen, it underwent only minor changes, notably the replacement of the windows by T-form ones, then in fashion.

The museum occupies five rooms on the first floor, known in Dutch as the 'bel-etage' or the 'fine-floor'. The great saloon still has its crystal chandelier and wall lights dating from 1790. Note the music room with its beautiful ceilings painted in 1870. The Belgian-style room, dating from 1866 and unchanged, is also worth a look.

The museum was created in 1990, after the renovation of the building by Bob Meijer, in memory of his ginger cat John Pierpont Morgan, named after the famous banker J.P. Morgan. The collections reveal the role of the cat in our world through the centuries, as depicted in paintings, drawings and sculptures by Pablo Picasso, Rembrandt, Henri de Toulouse-Lautrec and many others. Cat lover or art lover, you'll enjoy this unusual exhibition.

THE DIFFERENT TYPES OF GABLES

For the most part, the gables of houses are all different. Decorating the façades, they are there to mask the end of a classic pitched roof, a little like a theatre décor. Often of a very marked style, they reveal the period during which the house was built.

The oldest gables are called "stepped" (trapgevel).They date from the first part of the 17th century, a period when Renaissance style required the avoidance of diagonal lines, hence the need to hide the slopes of roofs, which were considered unattractive.

From 1615 to 1625, the baroque influence of the architect Hendrick de Keyser revealed itself through the appearance of stucco ornaments on this type of façade. Scrolls and statues added touches of white.

There are also several of these types of gables on certain 19th-century neo-Renaissance houses.

The gables of the more modest houses are called "spout" (tuitgevel). They were used between 1620 and 1720 to decorate modest houses and warehouses, also for the rear façades of houses having two façades, as at 14 Oudezijds Voorburgwal.

These gables resemble stepped gables that retained only the bottom and top steps.

The point of the gable is often decorated with carved stones.

The commonest gables are those called "bell" gables (klokgevel), and those called **"neck-gables"** (halsgevel).

They appeared in the second half of the 17th century under the influence of Classicism. The upper part of the façade is richly decorated with foliage, fruits and flowers in stucco, sometimes even sea-gods, nymphs and dolphins.

Even small attic windows and the hoisting beam were decorated. In the 18th century these remained the most common form of gable, but in a style which became more and more detailed, under the influence of Louis XIV, and later Louis XV.

The rich decoration of the gable was intended to proclaim the prosperity of the proprietor, by illustrating, for example, the towns or countries where he did business or presenting the arms of the family.

In the 18th and 19th centuries, the wealthiest houses adopted wide rectilinear gables (Rechte kroonlijsten ou Lijstgevel).

The cornices are mainly decorated with stucco mouldings representing birds or scrolls.

Maxims and proverbs are also a pleasing ornament.

In the middle of the 19th century there was a reversion to bell gables, and also to a refined version of cornices in the form of straight wooden ones.

Step-gable

Spout-gable

Neck-gable

Bell-gable

THE FRENCH STYLE GARDEN OF THE INSTITUT FRANCAIS ❼

Descartes House, Vijzelgracht 2A, 1017HR Amsterdam
• Tel.: 020 531 95 01
• Visit by request • Library open Monday, Tuesday and Thursday 12pm-3pm and 5pm-8pm, Wednesday 12pm-8pm, and Saturday 11am-5pm

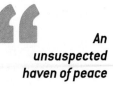

What a pleasure it is to discover this very lovely French-style garden hidden behind an imposing building, right alongside a noisy, busy street; its calm and beauty is conducive to meditation.

> *An unsuspected haven of peace*

For access, ask at the reception or visit the adjoining library.

Created in 1933 by Gustave Cohen, a professor at the Sorbonne in Paris, the Descartes House is an institution whose role is to promote French culture in The Netherlands. It was only in 1971, though, that it moved into this grand building.

Built between 1669 and 1671 by the architect Adriaan Dortsman, it is one of the largest buildings of the Golden Age. Its rather plain appearance, reflecting Dutch classical style, puts the emphasis on ideal classical proportions with wide, unified façade surfaces, rather than decorative motifs and pilasters.

The building was originally an orphanage for Walloon children, and remained so till 1967. Various traces of that time have been preserved, particularly the Regents' Room, the orphanage kitchen and a fine collection of paintings and books. The most surprising element is certainly the arrangement of the garden. This garden, re-styled in French fashion, matches the style of the building remarkably well.

RENE DESCARTES IN THE NETHERLANDS

An outstanding 17th-century figure, the French philosopher, mathematician, scientist and writer Rene Descartes is better known as one of the fathers of modern philosophy and mathematics than as a symbol of Franco-Dutch cultural exchange.

However, in 1618, in his quest to discover the world, he entered the service of the Dutch leader Maurice of Nassau, with the idea of pursuing a military career. He travelled in several European countries, but in 1624 returned to France, where he devoted himself to studying philosophy and the science of optics. In 1628, though, he sold his possessions and re-established himself in The Netherlands, both to take advantage of the great freedom of spirit he found there and to escape from the distractions of Paris. He lived in Amsterdam (see page 128), Deventer, Utrecht and Leiden.

It was certainly early during his stay in The Netherlands that Descartes wrote his major work 'The Philosophical Essays', published in 1637.

He left The Netherlands in 1649, persuaded by Queen Christina of Sweden to settle in Sweden. But the climate did not suit him and he died a few months later of pneumonia, on 26 February 1650.

HOLTKAMP'S CAKE AND PASTRY SHOP ❽

Holtkamp, Vijzelgracht 15 1017HM Amsterdam
• Open Monday to Friday 8:30am-6pm, Saturday 8:30am-5pm
• Tel.: 020 624 87 57

> *Confectioner by Royal appointment*

This small family-run cake and pastry shop, much favoured by lovers of prawn croquettes and apple tarts, is notable for its shop-fittings and for its history.

The first bakery of the Holtkamp family was founded in 1885 on this same spot. Then, in 1928, the son of the first baker commissioned Piet Kramer, a famous architect of the Amsterdam School, to fit out the shop in a modern style. His concept was to give the impression, upon entering the shop, of going into a sort of Ali Baba's cave, and he paid great attention to every detail. Varnished light oak was used for the fittings, with highlights provided by dark coromandel wood and stained glass.

Above the shelves, the walls are decorated in wave patterns, painted by Pieter den Besten.

The shop is very small, measuring less than 20m². By contrast, the kitchen behind is very large, as is the lower floor, enabling 35 people to work there.

Several years ago, Mr. Holtkamp passed the business down to his daughter and her husband Nico Meijles, who maintain the culinary expertise as well as the taste for the historic architecture.

Above the entry door, note the Arms of the Dutch Royal Family, indicating that the cake shop is an appointed supplier to the Court.

HOFLEVERANCIER: MORE THAN 400 OFFICIAL SUPPLIERS TO THE COURT

To obtain the status of official supplier to the Court, or 'Hofleverancier', a business has to satisfy certain conditions.

This distinction is a guarantee of quality as well as the soundness and continuity of the enterprise. It is a symbol of the respect and of the appreciation and confidence of the Sovereign towards the beneficiary. The firm has to be Dutch and to have existed for at least a hundred years, preferably under the same name.

The King or Queen grants the title 'Supplier to the Court', valid for 25 years and renewable.

About 400 firms can claim the distinction of suppliers to the Court, not only multinationals like KLM and Shell, but also bakers, jewellers, horticulturalists and interior designers.

This seal of approval is generally depicted by a shield with the Royal Arms over the door or window - as at Holtkamp or at Hajenius (see page 72) - and recognisable by the motto 'Je maintiendrai'.

THE HOUSES AT THE CORNER ❾
OF VIJZELGRACHT AND PRINSENGRACHT

Café-restaurant Myrabelle • Vijzelgracht 1, 1017HL Amsterdam
• Tel.: 020 624 41 09 • Open Monday
to Saturday from 12pm to 1am

It is difficult to believe that in the 1960s, this street corner was no more than waste ground protected by wire fencing. Vijzelgracht had become an important main street for traffic, as a result of a town plan which involved widening Vijzelstraat between 1917 and 1926, then filling in the Vijzelgracht canal in 1933. This evolution made the area attractive for development. The Bazel building was constructed in 1919. It was followed by the Carlton Hotel in 1929 and then the offices of ABN Bank in 1962. In 1973, the bank decided to enlarge its premises by constructing a complex between the Keizersgracht and the Prinsengracht. This project raised a general outcry against the threat of a town centre massed with buildings, congested with traffic by day and deserted by night. The bank was therefore obliged to reduce the number of floors of the building.

> *A 1971 block of houses classed as a Historic Monument*

The principal outcome of this movement was that the urban restoration association "Amsterdam Maatschappij tot Stadsherstel" developed a strategy of acquiring and restoring the eastern side of the avenue. The most spectacular of these restorations concerned the houses at Nos 1, 3 and 5 Vijzelgracht and Nos 646-648 Prinsengracht. Eleven apartments, two boutiques and a bar thus came into being in 1971, in buildings created in the style of earlier times, on the basis of old photographs. Without this will to retain some of the town's past charm, there would certainly have been another office block on this space.

Along the line of the planned subway, between the Central Station and the RAI Station passing Damrak, Rokin, Vijzelstraat and Ferdinand Bolsstraat in particular, one can see, at the first floor level of certain buildings, cubes containing a rotating laser. These are not in fact surveillance cameras but theodolites, instruments to measure possible movements of buildings during the construction of the metro. 84 units can sound an alert that stops the work at the slightest subsidence.

TO SEE NEARBY

THE PIPE MUSEUM ❿
Pijpenkabinet, Prinsengracht 488, 1017KH Amsterdam
• Open Wednesday to Saturday 12pm to 6pm • Entry charge
• Tel.: 020 421 17 79

Founded initially from the private collection of Don Duco, who began his collection in 1969 with pipes found during archaeological excavations in Amsterdam, the pipe museum has a collection of more than 20,000 pipes that is unique in Europe. Two thousand of them are displayed in the permanent collection. The museum also hosts a library with more than 4,000 books.

A TUNNEL UNDER THE KEIZERSGRACHT

As the ABN-Amro Bank needed to transport money regularly from the coffers of the new building to the strong rooms of their old building, a tunnel was created under the Keizersgracht.

It was nicknamed the "pennies tunnel" and should soon be open to visitors.

THE DUTCH TRADING COMPANY was founded in 1824 by King William I to re-stimulate the economy, which was then in decline. The Company's aim was to financially support international trade, especially with The Netherlands Indies, which at that time were colonies. During the 20th century, with the disappearance of the colonies, this organization took on the form of a traditional bank. But it was granted, by The Netherlands government, the sole right to ship the agricultural output of the colonies - mainly coffee, sugar and indigo- to The Netherlands and to sell them here.

The population of The Netherlands Indies became more and more exploited. In his book 'Max Havelaar', Edouard Douwes Dekker, who had worked in The Netherlands Indies, denounced the exploitation of the local population by the administrators of The Netherlands Indies. The word "Multatuli", which became his nickname, is Latin for "I have greatly suffered". (see page 115)

THE "DE BAZEL" BUILDING ⓫

Vijzelstraat 32, 1017HL Amsterdam
• Open Tuesday to Friday 10am to 5pm,
Saturday and Sunday 11am to 5pm
• Tel.: 020 251 18 00
• Guided visit on request • Entry charge

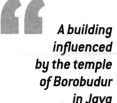

A building influenced by the temple of Borobudur in Java

Built in the 1920s for the Dutch Trading Company "Nederlandsche Handel-Maatschappij" (NHM, see opposite page), the building called "De Bazel" is named after its architect, Karel de Bazel.

Nicknamed "spekkoek" or "layer cake" by Amsterdammers, this building has the appearance of a succession of layers in two alternating colours; the concrete skeleton is covered with alternating red brick and light granite stone layers, following the example of the Buddhist Temple of Borobudur in Java, Indonesia. Born of a theosophical notion, and inspired by the American architects Frank Lloyd Wright and Louis Sullivan, the building doesn't adhere to any particular artistic school, but rather conveys a wider message, with the choice of numerous decorative elements reflecting myths and symbols. Harmony is contained in the principle of construction: the composition of the façade is based on a mathematical balance of rectangles in the proportion of 9 x 8. Finally, light, symbolizing the Divine, plays an important role in the building, which is built around two light-wells.

Bazel sought to achieve this spirit of harmony with both the exterior and the interior. Looking at the building as a whole, one can see some marvellous ornaments. Seen more closely, they actually hide a ventilation system designed to bring fresh air to the entire building. Bazel also developed a central vacuum-cleaning system as well as under-floor heating.

Like numerous architects at that time, Bazel thought that harmony and beauty should be found in everyday things. He applied great care to interior details, particularly floors, ceilings, painted wallpapers, windows and light-fittings. He went so far as to design some of the furniture and even an umbrella holder. Many of the building's decorations refer to the (former) colonies. On each side of the entrance is a statue of a woman: one, pensive, representing Asia, the other, alert, representing Europe. High up on the façade, three sculptures of Governors-General of the former Netherlands Indies can be seen. Finally, on the corners of the building are sculptures paying homage to traders and sailors.

At the end of the 1950s, the building on the south side of the Vijzelgracht started collapsing. ABN-Amro Bank, proprietors at that time, decided to replace these ruins by a "modern" building. Although one cannot compare the style, there are, however, similarities to the Bazel building in the façade and the upper section.

THE BOUTIQUE OF THE LITTLE LADIES ⓬

Tesselschade - Arbeid Adelt
Leidseplein 33, 1017PS Amsterdam
• Tel.: 020 623 66 65 • Open Tuesday to Friday 11am to 6pm,
Saturday 11am to 5pm

A shop dedicated to hand-made products

The Tesselschade-Arbeit Adelt association is the oldest women's association in The Netherlands. It exists not for its members but thanks to its members.

Since 1871, its vocation has been to help women and young girls in their quest for financial independence. For several years now, it has also had the objective of preserving craft skills. At the time of its creation, helping women become financially independent of their husbands was a rather revolutionary concept.

In actuality, the 34 local branches in The Netherlands, with the strength of their 11,000 members, support the craft/skills training of women who have difficulty earning a living. Once trained, their attractive products either help stock the shops or are sold privately.

In Amsterdam, the shop is run by volunteers who want to contribute to women's emancipation. They welcome you and help you choose from the articles made by 35 ladies, who augment their income thanks to the association. Here you can find, for example, hand-made smock dresses, delightful little hand-knitted bootees for babies, as well as those little bunny rabbits one finds in every Dutch nursery.

The shop gives you the feeling of delving into your grandmother's handwork box and finding little treasures at low prices.

"EVERYONE THEIR WHY"

The motto of the association is "elke zijn waarom" which means "everyone their why", in fact meaning that everyone has a good reason for wanting to earn her living thanks to the association.

AN AMUSING FIRST NAME...

Tesselschade was the second Christian name given by ship-owner Roemer Visser to his daughter Maria. On the day of her birth, one of her father's ships, returning to The Netherlands, came to grief on the Isle of Texel (schade in Dutch means damage). Note the names of the two streets on the other side of the Leidseplein towards the Vondelpark: Tesselschadestraat and Roemer Visserstraat.

WHY ARE THERE PIKES IN THE FOUNTAIN ON THE LEIDSEPLEIN ?

In front of the American Hotel is a splendid fountain, renovated in 2006, at the centre of which two large pikes spew out water. They owe their presence here to the fact that the renovation of the fountain was, for the most part, financed by an endowment from Madame Snoek ("Pike" in Dutch).

THE FORTY LIZARDS **13**
Kleine Gartmanplantsoen, 1017RP Amsterdam

On the little square called Kleine Gartmanplantsoen, forty sculptures of
lizards and iguanas creep around in the grass, amongst the daisies. The
creations of Hans van Houwelingen, these bronze sculptures were produced
in 1994. The reptiles are concentrated in two places: near the crossing toward
the Max Euweplein and close to the bridge over the Leidsegracht. These
lizards recall that, before 1913, the Lijnbaansgracht canal was located here.
Once it was covered over, the city theatre was built there, breaking the harmony
created by the structure of Amsterdam around the canals.

Why lizards? As they adapt to their environment and sometimes even adopt
the same colour, lizards are traditionally the symbol of eternal life; even if
they lose their tail, they do not die. This would seem to indicate that despite
its changes, the town retains its soul.

THE TREES OF THE LEYDE GATE **14**
Opposite Leidseplein, on the other side of the bridge, two very large trees
mark the spot where travellers tied their horses while they completed the
administrative formalities before entering the town by the Leidsepoort or
"the Leyde Gate", built in 1664 and demolished in 1826. The first American
Hotel was built on that location in 1881. It was completely rebuilt in 1902
in Art Nouveau style by the architects Willem Kromhout and H.G. Jansen.
The interior is still unchanged and is worth a look.

THE LADYBIRD OF NON-VIOLENCE **15**
Marnixstraat 401-403, 1017PJ Amsterdam

On Marnixstraat between the "Lux" and "Kamer 401" bars, is a paving
stone with a ladybird, placed here after a gratuitous act of violence. It is,
like several other equivalent plaques, a witness of the past and a daily appeal
for non-violence.

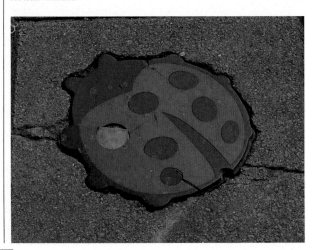

THE STATUE OF THE LITTLE WOODCUTTER ⑯
Leidsebosje, Stadhouderskade 12, 1054ES Amsterdam

In this square just across the bridge from the Leidseplein, one can spot a surprising little statue in the trees, representing a man in the process of sawing through the branch supporting him. This anonymous piece of art has been here since 1989.

THE MAX EUWE MUSEUM ⑰
Max Euweplein 30a, 1017MB Amsterdam
• Tel.: 020 625 70 17 • Open Tuesday to Friday 12pm to 4pm, and the first Saturday of each month

The Max Euwe Museum is dedicated to the greatest chess player The Netherlands has ever known. The fifth player to be crowned World Chess Champion, in 1935, Max Euwe was born near Amsterdam in 1901 and studied and taught mathematics. Fascinated by the intuitional approach to chess, he wrote more than 70 books on the theory of the subject, of which a number are available in the museum. The museum retraces his career as well as his contribution to the history of chess. Apart from the chess-related personal effects of Max Euwe, you can admire unique chess sets from around the world. Also, the museum contains a large collection of photographs of chess tournaments. Outside, at ground level, is a large chessboard with giant pieces for passers-by to play.

THE FRANKENDAEL RESIDENCE

Middenweg 72, 1097BS Amsterdam
- Visit on Sunday 11am-12pm and on request 020 423 39 30
- Restaurant Merckelbach 020 665 08 80
- De Kas 020 462 45 62

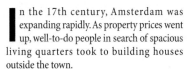

> *A gentleman's residence from the Golden Age turned into a public park*

I n the 17th century, Amsterdam was expanding rapidly. As property prices went up, well-to-do people in search of spacious living quarters took to building houses outside the town.

The Frankendael house, set in 7 hectares of land, is the last example of these lovely homes, used as summer residences by wealthy merchants. In 1629, a new polder, the Watergraafsmeer, was created to the southeast of Amsterdam following the drying out of the Diemermeer Lake. Forty residences were constructed in the area, including this one, built in 1695 by Izaak Baalde. He called it Frankendael, to recall Franckenthull, the little German village from which his father had fled religious persecution.

The entrance to the park is through a grille set into a monumental wooden door in the style of Louis XIV. On the gable above, one can see a medallion representing the winged helmet of Mercury, from the arms of Jacob Otten Husky, the owner at the time the door was made. On the back is the date of construction, 1783, in Roman numerals. The park, which was restored in 2004, contains several gardens, including one created around 1730 in French Regency style. An arboretum contains nearly 500 different varieties of trees, including a superb row of limes dating from 1905, a very fine oak and a lovely Japanese sophora. In the front of the

house, there is a marble fountain dating from 1714. It was originally created for the town of Driemond, which is situated within the confines of three rivers. They are represented here by allegorical figures: the Greek gods Poseidon and Amphitrite mix the waters, like the merging of the Gaasp and the Gein, while a young lute player seated on a dolphin joins in, like the little Smalweesp river.

At the bottom of the park, the greenhouse is used as a restaurant, serving dishes prepared from vegetables grown in the garden.

THE LOWEST POINT OF THE TOWN
This Watergraafsmeer area is the lowest point of Amsterdam, being 6.2 meters below the NAP.

RE-CREATION OF A CANAL
Aquarium of the Artis Zoo • Plantage Kerklaan 38-40, 1018CZ Amsterdam
• Open daily from 9am to 5pm, and to 6pm in the summer • Entry charge
• Tel.: 0900 278 47 96

Even though it is clearly forbidden, using the canals for dumping is an ingrained habit of Amsterdammers. One way to see the extent of this is to wait for a very harsh winter when the canals are frozen. Old mattresses and bicycle frames become visible through the transparent ice. The other way is to visit the amusing re-creation in the aquarium of the Artis Zoo.

This cross section of a canal from top to bottom, from the level of car wheels in the street to the bottom of the water, is very realistic, thanks to the presence of details like an old car wheel clamp and a bike.

WATER FOR AN AQUARIUM FROM THE GULF OF GASCONY
The seawater in the aquarium of the Artis Zoo has, since 1882, been transported by ship from the Bay of Gascony in the Atlantic Ocean. Thanks to the currents of the Gulf Stream, the water from this location is of very good quality, and only needs to be replaced once a year. 165,000 tons are shipped in each year.

POLLUTION OF THE CANAL WATER
The pollution of the water in Amsterdam is a subject as old as the town itself. By the Middle Ages, town regulations forbade the throwing of dead animals or dung into the water. The first attempt to bring fresh water into the canals dates from the 17th century, with the digging of the Nieuwe Vaart canal to the River IJ. Unfortunately, the difference in levels was not enough to ensure a sufficient flow of water.

In 1866 Amsterdam experienced a serious cholera epidemic that claimed numerous victims.

The foul quality of the water was identified as the main cause, and in 1867 the Amsterdam Health Board commissioned an engineer named C. Outshoorn to produce a plan for cleansing the water. In particular, he proposed that the Singelgracht should be used as a clean water reservoir, but his plan was never executed. Instead, the system still in use today was instituted, which consists of flushing the water out of the canals into the North Sea Canal and replacing it with clean water from the IJsselmeer, twice a week in winter and four times a week in summer. Fourteen locks are opened for this operation, on the Singelgracht and the Stadhouderskade. The water is propelled by powerful electric pumps at Zeeburg with a capacity of 3,400 cubic meters a minute. The problem was substantially resolved by the end of the 20th century, all the canal-side houses having been connected to the drains by the 1980s.

THE CITADEL BY BERLAGE

Vakbondsmuseum, Henri Polaklaan 9 1018CP Amsterdam
• Visit on request by phoning 020 624 11 66 • Entry charge

The little Trade Union Museum (Vakbondsmuseum) helps one understand the specific nature of the Dutch unions, which, unlike their European cousins, have always played the card of compromise, positioning themselves politically in the centre.

A superb example of the architecture of the Amsterdam School

The building was constructed for the Diamond Workers Union (ANDB) in 1903 by the architect Hendrik Berlage in the very recognizable style of the Amsterdam School (see page 270).

Numerous symbols from the world of diamonds were used as motifs in the decoration. Berlage, who had travelled considerably in Italy, drew his inspiration from Italian town halls of the Middle Ages: very large buildings with plain flat façades. Here, the only decorative features are the initials of the union.

Berlage wanted to give this building the character of a workers' citadel and the building truly has the character of a fortress, with its thick walls and a tower typical of this architectural style. The exterior decoration is achieved through the interplay of bricks and stones of different colours. The monumental entry hall creates a theatrical effect, with the mix of glazed bricks of different hues and the light fittings designed by Jan Eisenloeffel.

In the meeting rooms on the first floor, one can't miss the Art Nouveau pictures by Richard and Henriette Roland Holst. Between 1904 and 1907, they produced three paintings, representing the past, present and future of the Socialist movement. As the paintings soon started to deteriorate, it was decided to cover them with panels and repaint them. In 1937, nine new illustrations were created and completed.

The decoration of the management office on the second floor was donated by young union members after the successful negotiation of an 8-hour day for diamond workers in 1911. These three paintings by R. Roland Holst date from 1912 and represent the three ideal moments in the life of the working man: the vigorous hours of work, the pleasant hours of rest and the deep hours of sleep.

THE PLANT DOCTOR

21

Hortus Botanicus, Plantage Middenlaan 2A, 1018DD Amsterdam
• Wednesdays between 1pm and 2pm
• Tel.: 020 625 90 21

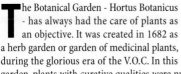

Personal advice on caring for your plants

The Botanical Garden - Hortus Botanicus - has always had the care of plants as an objective. It was created in 1682 as a herb garden or garden of medicinal plants, during the glorious era of the V.O.C. In this garden, plants with curative qualities were nurtured. Exotic plants brought back by the V.O.C. ships from the Far East were also conserved here.

Currently, the collection contains 6,000 plants, representing more than 4,000 species from all over the world.

The gardeners are also at your service. Have a sick plant? Ask the plant doctor who advises every Wednesday from 1pm to 2pm. Bring your plant, a leaf or a flower, or even a photo, and he will suggest ways to cure its ills. The service can also be consulted by phone at 020 625 90 21 or by e-mail: plantendokter@dehortus.nl.

In the furthest greenhouse, you can admire an exceptional collection of cycads. One of them, of the Encephalartos Altensteinii variety, is the oldest potted plant in the world. Over the past 300 years it has grown to a height of more than 4.5 metres. And don't miss the café restaurant situated in the Orangery with its lovely terrace, in the middle of the garden.

TO SEE NEARBY

THE MOTHERS' HOUSE

22

Hubertus House, Plantage Middenlaan 33-35, 1018DB Amsterdam

Built in 1973, this 6-floor 'home' was designed by the architect Aldo van Eyck (see also p239), in the modernist tradition of Dutch 20th-century architecture. It was designed to bring warmth and comfort to the parents and children of the single-parent families who live there. The architecture provides a feeling of rediscovered intimacy, thanks to the central staircase, terraces and passages. The great expanses of glass and the use of all the colours of the rainbow give the place a light and cheerful atmosphere.

THE "AUSCHWITZ NEVER AGAIN" MONUMENT ㉓

Wertheimpark, Plantage Middenlaan, 1018DE Amsterdam

The monument of broken mirrors

The monument of broken mirrors, created in 1977 in memory of the victims of Auschwitz by Dutch artist Jan Wolkers, has been located in the lovely Wertheimpark since 1993.

During the Second World War, 67 trains left The Netherlands, deporting nearly 60,000 Dutch Jews to the Auschwitz-Birkenau camp and 34,000 to the one in Sobibor. 1,150 returned from the former and only 19 from the latter. In January 1952, the Polish Government organised the first commemoration of the liberation of the Auschwitz camp. The Netherlands delegation of survivors brought back a funerary urn that was interred beneath a commemorative plaque in the Eastern Cemetery or "Oosterbegraafplaats."

In 1977, the plaque was replaced by a work comprising six plaques of fissured glass. The artist wanted to convey that, since the Holocaust, the image of the sky, as seen in the cracked glass, is no longer blue and clear. In 1993 the monument was moved to the Wertheimpark.

Each year, a silent procession takes place here, on the last Sunday of January, to commemorate the liberation of Auschwitz (27 January 1945).

Where the Wertheimpark is now situated, there used to be one of the oldest parks in Amsterdam, created in 1812. Only one small green space, less than one hectare, was retained and renamed in 1898 after the banker, politician, aesthete and philanthropist Abraham Wertheim (1832-1897). A monumental fountain was erected in his honour.

A DIGITAL MEMORIAL FOR THE JEWS OF AMSTERDAM
The website www.joodsmonument.nl is a new form of memorial. On the welcome page of this innovative website, each tiny square represents a Jewish person who was deported: a blue square for a man, red for a woman, green for a boy and yellow for a girl.
By clicking on these small squares, one discovers the identity of each of these thousands of people and their address before deportation.

TO SEE NEARBY

(24)

THE DUTCH THEATRE, A MEMORIAL TO THE DEPORTED JEWS

Hollandse Schouwburg, Plantage Middenlaan 24, 1018DE Amsterdam
• Open daily from 11am to 4pm • Tel.: 020 531 03 40

Today, behind its impressive façade, nothing can be seen of the former glory of this theatre's history of entertainment. It is, instead, a poignant memorial to the Jews who were deported during WWII. In 1892, inspired by his travels, the architect Bombach built the Dutch Theatre in a neo-Renaissance style, newly in vogue in Amsterdam.

Built opposite the Artis Zoo, in the middle of the Plantage neighbourhood, it was the fourth most important theatre in this area, although far from being the largest or most luxurious. The entrance gave access to a great white marble hall, which led to the 1,360 seats in the orchestra, boxes and balconies.

When it opened in 1892, under the name of the Artis Theatre, operettas were performed there. In the face of competition, particularly from the Frascati theatre, it went bankrupt. Two years later, it re-opened under the name Dutch Theatre, mainly for dramatic performances. In 1930 it was renovated by Wolter Bakker, who reduced the number of seats to 750 and installed electric lighting. Unfortunately, this failed to ward off a second bankruptcy in 1938. The theatre then became the Plaza and put on popular shows in the style of American revues.

Under the German occupation, in October 1941, its name was changed again: it became 'The Jewish Theatre'. Under the law of 15 September 1941, which forbade Jews to assemble in public places, this theatre became the only place where Jewish artists could perform for a Jewish public. Existing effectively at the very centre of Jewish life, it became the location for Jewish weddings, which were no longer allowed at the Town Hall. In August 1942, the theatre was requisitioned by the occupying forces as the assembly place for Jews before their deportation. Up to 1,300 people were crowded into the premises for several days before being deported. Between 60,000 and 80,000 Jews left for the Dutch transit camps of Vught and Westerbork in this manner.

After the war, the theatre was used by its new leaseholders, Piccadilly Theatre, to put on a few private shows. But their wish to resume public entertainment unleashed an outcry and led to the formation of an association that, from 1946, raised the funds needed to buy the building. It was handed over to the Amsterdam municipality on the sole condition that it never again be used for entertainment but for remembrance, and this was achieved between 1958 and 1962. Only the façade was preserved, while the auditorium was replaced by an open courtyard. A memorial obelisk was erected where the stage used to be. The entry hall leads to a chapel where a perpetual flame burns in memory of the deceased, and one can read the 6,700 family names of the 104,000 Jews who were deported from The Netherlands.

THE BASEMENT OF THE CARRÉ ROYAL THEATRE ㉕

Amstel 115-125, 1018EM Amsterdam
• Guided visits on Saturdays • Entry charge
• Tel.: 0900 25 25 255

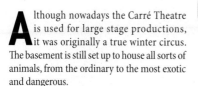

*A true
winter circus*

Although nowadays the Carré Theatre is used for large stage productions, it was originally a true winter circus. The basement is still set up to house all sorts of animals, from the ordinary to the most exotic and dangerous.

The Carré Theatre takes its name not from its shape (carré = square), but from the name of its founder Oscar Carré, a German circus artist, who was also a shrewd businessman and who built his fortune through his circus.

In 1863, his father, Wilhelm Carré, went to Amsterdam to put on his first equestrian show at the time of a fair. These shows rapidly became so popular that he sought to set himself up on a permanent basis in Amsterdam. He was only given a temporary permit at first, and built a wooden structure for his circus on land near the Amstel. Lengthy negotiations with the town council followed, as he attempted to retain and enlarge this wooden theatre; it was considered dangerous, due to the risk of fire.

Finally, in 1886, Oscar Carré obtained permanent authorisation, which enabled him to construct a theatre building. This was rapidly undertaken, in neo-Renaissance style.

The performance hall was arranged as an amphitheatre that could seat 2,000 people under a 26m high top.

The Oscar Carré circus troop went on tour during the summer months and the hall was leased for other events. Bit by bit, variety shows superseded circus performances. Oscar Carré's health declined, and the circus gave its last performance here in April 1909, not very long before his death in 1911, in Copenhagen, where the circus was on tour.

In 1991, the theatre underwent a major renovation. From a grand circus arena with only a small theatre, it became a large theatre with only a small area related to the circus. In the basement you can still see the stables and other stalls for the animals, which have been preserved as they used to be.

To mark the centenary of its construction, the theatre was given the title "Royal" or "Koninklijk" (see page 175).

While the theatre roof is constructed from timber, the impressive metal structure of its dome was the work of Gustav Eiffel. During the most recent renovation of the building, the interior of the dome, previously just basic lofts, was fitted out so that this space is now an elegant foyer, where dinners and receptions can be held.

THE ENTRANCE DOOR OF THE BESJESHUIS ㉖

Museum Hermitage Amsterdam, Amstel 51, 1001 GR Amsterdam
• Tel.: 020 530 87 55 • Open daily from 10am to 5pm, Wednesday till 8pm
• Restaurant Neva, open Tue-Sat from 10am-11pm, Monday and Sunday
10am-6pm

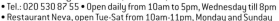

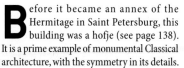

Before it became an annex of the Hermitage in Saint Petersburg, this building was a hofje (see page 138). It is a prime example of monumental Classical architecture, with the symmetry in its details.

A door that has never been opened

It was built by Hans Petersom between 1681 and 1683, on the banks of the Amstel, on a plot of land surrounded by three streams of water: the Nieuwe Herengracht, the Nieuwe Keizersgracht and the Amstel river. Originally, the building was a home welcoming elderly women; men were accepted after 1719. It was known as the Besjeshuis or Amstelhof. After three centuries of use as a hospice for close to 700 residents, it was closed in 2007, the last boarders having moved to more modern institutions. An extensive renovation and restructuring then began, organized by the architect Hans van Heeswijk.

Since its construction, the main façade has faced the river and features three major doors placed in a stone frame. The two doors on the sides were used as main entrances to the building by the regents, but the one in the middle was installed here, at the top of a few stairs, for the sole purpose of harmony: it has never been opened. Behind this door is a vast room with an organ, used as a church by the hospice. Today, it is a venue for concerts, especially on Sundays.

This room has also been used several times on major occasions - as a ball room in 1814 for the reception following the return of King Willem I from England, for instance, and later, to celebrate Churchill's visit in 1946 and for the opening of the new museum in 2009 attended by Queen Beatrix, Prince Willem-Alexander, Princess Maxima and the Russian president Dmitri Medvedev. Under the staircase, there is another door. It gives access to the garden of the Hermitage, redesigned in a modern style by landscaper Michael van Gessel and interior designer Evelyne Merkx.

The Besjeshuis was already in existence when Peter the Great of Russia visited Amsterdam in 1685. It was only much later, in 2009, that this block of 4,400 square meters was converted into a Russian art heritage museum.

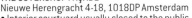

TO SEE NEARBY

THE COVERSHOF FAÇADE

Nieuwe Herengracht 4-18, 1018DP Amsterdam
• Interior courtyard usually closed to the public

A liturgical center belonging to the Protestant community of Amsterdam, the Corvershof was a foundation reporting to the Reformed Deaconry*. Single men and women would live in the Amstelhof, but the Covershof was dedicated to old couples with no children. Built in 1722 by the architect Steven Vennecool and recently renovated, it is a colossal building of 3 stories, with an interior courtyard and attic. The basement is still in use today as a wine shop. The pediment is decorated with a representation of the Covershof project: an allegory of charity in the beak of an eagle. Under the pediment, on the façade, notice the three baskets ("corven") and the three sandals ("trippen"), the arms of the individuals who donated money for the construction: Joan Corver (1688-1719) and Sara Maria Trip (1693-1721).

A poem in Dutch by Mattheus Brouërius van Nidek is written above the door. It honours the founders: "If charity needs to be thanked for and the support to the poor rewarded, the name of Corver and Trip comes on every tongue like honey. Thanks to their gift and their will, this house of God was built, the building shows their coat of arms, and their name will remain for ever."

A SURPRISING RECONSTRUCTION OF AN HISTORIC BUILDING THAT'S ONLY 20 YEARS OLD

It is almost impossible for someone who is not aware to realize that the buildings at Nos 45-55 on Nieuwe Herengracht are brand new. They were rebuilt with special care to the original design. The buildings of the Waterleiding (the water company) were previously located here.

Due to the excavations for the subway construction, several buildings became fragile and even collapsed.

In 1972, the decision was made to pull down the last houses at Nos 47, 49 and 51, with the intention to rebuild them later.

To respect the historic monument, measurements were taken and raw materials that could be reused were stored.

Only in 1993, after local quarrels were solved and financing found, did reconstruction start. The gables look like they did before.

Though the interior is now made of concrete, the staircases are the same as they used to be. It took more than 20 years to close this architectural gap, but the result is pretty amazing.

---

* Deaconry : Protestant service for poor and sick people

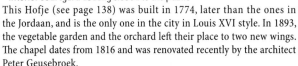

TO SEE NEARBY

OCCO HOFJE

Nieuwe Keizersgracht 94, 1018DS Amsterdam

• Interior courtyard usually closed to the public

This Hofje (see page 138) was built in 1774, later than the ones in the Jordaan, and is the only one in the city in Louis XVI style. In 1893, the vegetable garden and the orchard left their place to two new wings. The chapel dates from 1816 and was renovated recently by the architect Peter Geusebroek.

This Hofje was founded thanks to the legacy of Cornelia Elisabeth Occo. This businesswoman was the heir of the merchant and banker Pompejus Occo, and was single. She was well integrated in the business

world in Paris, London and Brussels: she owned shares of the French "Compagnie des Indes", for instance. In 1752, she mentioned in her testament that her patrimony should be used to build a hofje for poor widows and single elderly women. The building was set up to welcome 33 residents, the same number as the age of Christ, who all had to be Catholic. On the front of the building, on top of the pediment, is written "'t Gebouw van Barmhartigheid" (the building of charity). The eagle, which belongs to the Occo family coat of arms, is used in the decoration, outside on the façade, inside and even at the end of the stair handrail.

VAN BRANTS RUSHOFJE

Nieuwe Keizersgracht 38-40, 1018DS Amsterdam

• Interior courtyard usually closed to the public

Christofel Brants was the son of a barrel-maker from Eastern Friesland. He traded with Russia and got special attention from Peter the Great's entourage, which lead him to welcome him during his visits to Amsterdam in 1716. The following year, the tsar conferred a title of nobility on him. Brants was single and decided to have a hofje (see page 138) built in 1731 by the architect Daniël Marot. He died the following year but left a significant part of his patrimony to complete the construction.

The result is an impressive building with 3 floors, basement, attic and a charming courtyard. Above the entry cornice, a poem is written and says in short: "follow Brants in his virtues and his Love for the poor". The coat of arms of the founder can be seen in the middle section; they represent a red star with six branches. Above the cornice, a relief represents Charity, surrounded by indigent women. In the garden, the façade is one level lower than the street. Notice the swan surrounded by angels in the middle of the garden, symbolizing Brant's Lutheran faith (see page 111).

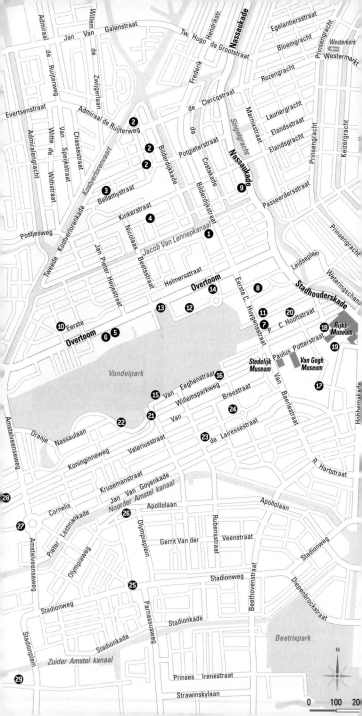

SOUTH - VONDELPARK

AN INDOOR SKI SLOPE ❶

Ski-inn Amsterdam, W.G. Plein 281, 1054SE Amsterdam
• Tel.: 020 607 01 48
• Ski lessons by appointment

*A ski slope
in the heart
of the city*

In the middle of the W.G. Terrain housing complex, in the main room that formerly housed the university hospital's amphi-theatre, is a surprising indoor ski slope that can cater for 4 skiers.

It uses an ingenious system of conveyer belts, which gradually "pulls" the skier upward as he descends the slope. The speed of the belt can be adjusted to suit the skier's level of expertise. Nevertheless, the installation is more appropriate for learning than for perfecting one's skills.

THE HISTORY OF THE W.G. TERREIN

In the 16th century, the W.G. Terrein was situated outside the city. The location was particularly appropriate to welcome a hospital. With the expansion of the city in the following centuries, it became necessary to build a large hospital, a counterpart to the OLVG located in the heart of the city.

In 1891, 10-year-old Princess Wilhemina laid the first stone of the Wilhemina Gasthuis (W.G.). Rebuilt after a fire in 1925, it was then the biggest hospital in The Netherlands, with 1700 beds in 20 wings, a university of medicine, and a nursing school.

As the town continued to expand and medicine to evolve, a new university hospital, the A.M.C. (Amsterdams Medisch Centrum) was built in 1980 to replace the Wilhemina Gasthuis, which was closed in 1983.

The municipality bought the area but had to change its plans due to protest from locals, especially the artists who had settled in some of the buildings and had created an association. In 1985, the W.G. Terrein foundation signed a contract of administration with the town. From then and till the end of the 1990s, the buildings were gradually rehabilitated, while preserving the spirit of the neighbourhood: a green and open district, combining both social and functional features. You can find housing, but also business incubators and leisure centres.

This rehabilitation highly respects the historic and cultural aspect of the area, adding great interest to this village within the town.

TO SEE NEARBY

CERAMIC PAINTINGS

Bellamyplein 22/38, 1053AT Amsterdam
Elisabeth Wolffstraat 59, 1052RN Amsterdam
Admiraal de Ruyterweg 52-80, 1056GM Amsterdam

In this working-class neighbourhood of rather ordinary brick buildings constructed in 1904, you should take a closer look at the building entrances, also called porticos.

Admire the surprising ceramic paintings illustrating typical scenes of Dutch life. These country scenes and seascapes are reproductions of classical 17th-century paintings. Of particular note are a representation of the city of Harlingen and the boat the "Halve Maen."

THE FORMER CHOCOLATE FACTORY

The imposing building on the Bellamystraat, at Nos 89-93, is a former chocolate factory founded by Caspar Flick in 1745 and taken over by Jan Dekker in 1799. It bore the name "Erven Caspar Flick & co".

Their specialty was the "flikje", a name still used today to refer to a delicate sugared chocolate sweet..

SCULPTURE OF THE THREE WINDBAGS

Corner of van de Borgerstraat and Ten Katestraat, 1053BV Amsterdam

This modern iron and bronze sculpture is an anonymous work of art from 1995. Three little men sitting on tall chairs appear to be having an intense conversation.

JOHANNA PARK   ❺
Overtoom 351-353, 1054 JA Amsterdam

Hidden along the busy Overtoom thoroughfare behind a door opposite the Staringstraat, one does not find a park, as its name might suggest, but instead a little back-alley that is home to six small, simple houses. In 1878, this modest neighbourhood was given the rather cynical name of "Johanna Park."

THE VAN GENDT STABLES   ❻
Overtoom 371-373, 1054 JA Amsterdam

The lovely houses of this little alley were built in 1876 by Adolf Van Gendt, to host stables, a blacksmith's workshop and some offices. Long left abandoned, then squatted, they were renovated by the Kentie architectural firm in 2003-04, and thus rediscovered their original end-of-the-19th-century character. Today, the small complex includes six dwellings, two shops, two offices, and the Spijker villa, a home for disabled children. At the beginning of the alley, notice the tramway rails in the pavement; they were used when the tramway was pulled by horses (see page 229).

SCULPTURES UNDER THE VIADUCT   ❼
At the level of Van Baerlestraat 1, 1071 AX Amsterdam

Walkers and cyclists in the Vondelpark usually hurry under this viaduct, which is the gateway between the park and the heart of the city. It's a shame to rush as in the middle of the underpass, under the arches on each side, are interesting sculptures by Hildo Krop carved in 1947 and renovated in 2009. They represent young parents taking a walk.

UNITED EUROPE ❽

Verenigd Europa, Roemer Visscherstraat 20-30a,
1054EX Amsterdam

> *Europe of architecture*

On the occasion of the Universal Exhibition in Antwerp in 1894, the architect Tjeerd Kuipers built seven adjoining houses in this quiet street, illustrating the architectural styles of seven countries in Europe.

At number 20, the house is built in German Romantic style. The house at number 22 resembles a Loire Valley château. The one next door is in a Moorish style reminiscent of southern Spain. The one at number 26 is a small Italian-style "palazzo". At number 28, the Russian house resembles a Russian cathedral from the time of Ivan the Terrible, with its dome-shaped roof adorned with a cross. The next house is built in Dutch Renaissance style. Last, to conclude the row, the English house resembles a little cottage.

TO SEE NEARBY

THE BIGGEST PAINTED WALL IN AMSTERDAM ❾
At the corner of Jacob van Lennepstraat and Nassaukade

It took almost three weeks for Rombout Oomen to finish the biggest painted wall in Amsterdam. It represents a man rushing toward a naked woman symbolizing Spring. The entire painting is covered by an erotic poem celebrating Spring, "aan een roosje" by Van Lennep. It's an amusing little story, but the sight of this woman's sex created so much controversy that, in 2004, the painting was modified to blur this part of her body.

RHYMES ON THE SIDEWALKS ❿
At the crossing of Eerste Helmersstraat and Rhijnvis Feithstraat,
Rhijnvis Feithstraat 21, Pieter Langendijkstraat 54, Brederodestraat 124

The streets just north of the Overtoom may not seem particularly poetic at first glance, but discerning eyes will notice small ceramic tiles embedded in the sidewalk, a letter on each one. Assembled, these letters form poems, and each poem's title can be found, on a larger tile, at the end of the verse.

THE REMAINS OF OTHER UNIVERSAL EXHIBITIONS IN AMSTERDAM

Amsterdam hosted two other universal exhibitions. The French entrepreneur Edouard Agostini, who also organized the exhibition in France in 1878, organized the first one in 1883. Of the temporary buildings, only a gate that has been used for the entrance of the Vondelpark on the Stadhouderskade remains.

During this exhibition, the Heineken brewery was awarded the "Diplome d'Honneur", which is still mentioned today in red on the bottles. Nothing remains of the exhibition hosted in 1913.

THE DUTCH FEMINIST MOVEMENT

The Dutch Feminist movement began to make a name for itself in the 1860s. The important women's liberation issues, such as working conditions, access to education for girls and matrimonial law, entered the realm of public debate. In 1894, the women's suffrage association ("Vereeniging voor Vrouwenkiesrecht") began lobbying for the recognition of women's civil rights.

In 1898, a large exhibition about working women, fashioned after the universal exhibitions that were so popular during the period, was organized in The Hague.

This marked the emergence of women into the Dutch public sphere and generated sizeable profits, allowing for the creation of a national office for working women that continued to support their actions. It took roughly twenty more years before Dutch women finally won the right to vote in 1919.

THE AMSTERDAM SCHOOL OF HOME ECONOMICS

❶

Amsterdamsche Huishoudschool, Zandpad 5, 1054GA Amsterdam
• StayOkay Youth Hostel
• Tel.: 020 589 89 96

> *Learning sewing, cleaning and cooking...*

This beautiful building has always been dedicated to youth. It has housed a youth hostel since 1972, but first opened in 1895 as a school of home economics.

At the end of the 19th century, it became possible to attend school to learn sewing, cooking, cleaning and washing as domestic sciences. These schools had two purposes: to train housemaids, and to prepare young ladies for their future household management tasks. This approach to domestic responsibility may seem sexist today, but it was actually quite progressive at the time. Its aim was to help emancipate women by transforming usual chores into paid work.

The Amsterdam School of Home Economics was founded by Johanna Naber and Jeltje de Bosch Kemper, two key feminist figures from the end of the century. Both came from the Protestant aristocracy. The first was the author of various books on the history of feminism; the second was known for her initiatives promoting work for women. She was on the board of directors of the Tesselschade association (see page 181).

In those days, schools of home economics published their own cookbooks; the first one here was published in 1910. Named after its author, Miss C.J. Wannée, the "Wannée-Kookboek" was reprinted for the 27th time in 2005.

In the 1970s, the nearby Vondelpark became the place for the Hippies in Europe to gather. "Fly K.L.M., sleep in the Vondelpark" was the national airline's advertising slogan. It reached the point that the town set up showers and toilets, luggage lockers and even a free coffee bar. Up to 85,000 people slept outdoors in Amsterdam during that period.

In 1972, the town decided to sell the home economics school building to the "Stayokay" company, which opened a youth hostel with more than 500 beds in 1975.

Since then, sleeping in the Vondelpark has been forbidden, as is clearly stated on the signs at the park entrances.

The name of Zandpad street ("Sandtpad" at the end of the 17th century) is a homage to the past. The name "pad" in Dutch ("path") was used for the small alleys that led into town. At the time, this location was outside the fortifications of the city, in an area where beautiful countryside residences were built.

THE CAFÉ AT THE DUTCH HORSE ARENA ⑫

Hollandsche manege, Vondelstraat 140, 1054GT Amsterdam
• Tel.: 020 618 09 42 • Open Monday to Friday from 10am to 1pm,
Saturday from 8am to 8pm and Sunday from 8am to 5pm
• Keep quiet in the arena and on the balcony of the café
• Ask permission of the stable-lads if you want to visit the stables
• Entry charge

*A timeless
atmosphere*

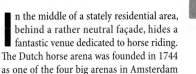

I n the middle of a stately residential area, behind a rather neutral façade, hides a fantastic venue dedicated to horse riding. The Dutch horse arena was founded in 1744 as one of the four big arenas in Amsterdam in the 18th century. It was originally situated on the Lijnbaansgracht around the Leidsegracht. In 1881, as its location blocked city development plans, the mayor decided to have it moved to a new plot of land, 2700 square meters in size, located between the Vondelstraat and the Vondelkade (currently Overtoom).

The city entrusted the construction of the building to architect Adolf Van Gendt in 1882. Both impressive and unique, the arena was built in a Renaissance style, strongly inspired by the Spanish Riding School of Vienna. Registered as a National Monument, it was renovated in 1986.

In order to have an entrance on the Vondelpark side, the municipality also bought the house at No 140 Vondelstraat. The building was preserved and is home to the manager of the riding school. The garden was used to provide access to the arena itself. This explains the large carriage entrance, finely decorated with stucco, in the middle of a street where mainly beautiful brick residences stand.

The arched corridor has a high ceiling and stucco ornaments, giving it a majestic, theatrical feel. It leads to two heavy wooden doors that open on to the arena itself and its timeless atmosphere. The walls of the arena are embellished with stucco, providing the illusion of cut stone.

The fantastic acoustic of the room, which amplifies the voices of the trainers, contributes to the arena's rather unique atmosphere.

Beyond the arena, around fifty horses and ponies wait quietly in the stables for the riding students.

Do not hesitate to go up the large staircase that leads to the foyer. The draperies, the ceiling decorated with stucco and the sculpted wood panelling create an elegant and sophisticated atmosphere. In this decor, one could expect to find women in elegant dresses, such as during the intermission of an opera, instead of the horse riders who are simply relaxing after a bit of riding.

Behind the arena, near No 169 on the Overtoom, columns have been erected to symbolize the location of houses demolished in 1980. Formerly, the arena was completely inserted in this housing block.

THE LOVELY HOUSES ON VONDELSTRAAT ⑬

Villa Nieuwe Leyerhoven, Vondelstraat 73-75, 1054GK Amsterdam
Villa Betty, Overtoom 241-245, 1054HV Amsterdam

A grass tennis court in the back garden

The houses on the south side of Vondel Street were built on land that was originally part of the Vondelpark. This first housing development helped finance the park.

The creation of the Vondelpark resulted from an initiative by a group of wealthy Amsterdammers, in particular Christiaan Pieter van Eeghen. Together they decided to create a park for walking and riding (a 'Rij- en Wandelpark') inspired by the great English parks, instead of the gas-works that the town of Amsterdam wanted to put there.

In 1867, Louis Royer's statue of the poet Vondel was erected in the new park, but it wasn't until 1880 that the park was officially named after the poet.

This private association was able to buy 16 hectares of land that was then developed by the architect David Zocher.

More land was bought in the following years to achieve a total of 48 hectares in 1877, a size that has remained unchanged ever since. To finance this enlargement, the association decided to sell a strip of land on the north side of the park. Some lovely houses, opening directly onto the park, were built in 1877 by the well-known architect Pierre Cuypers.

Don't miss the chance to take a look at the Nieuwe Leyerhoven house, where Cuypers lived until 1881. This house had its coach-house on Overtoom, at No 373. Another impressive residence is the Betty House, which derives its name from Betty von Hunteln who lived there

at the beginning of the century. Hidden behind a large entrance gate is an imposing house with numerous windowed verandas and a grass tennis court, all of which earned Betty the nickname 'Queen of the Overtoom'.

These houses were extremely posh, but the smart part of the town continued to develop on the south side of the park. There, the entrances have fine iron gates, while the more modest entrances on the north side denote a district intended for the less affluent population of the western district.

THE CURIOUS FINANCING OF THE VONDEL CHURCH

Vondelkerk • Vondelstraat 120, 1054GK Amsterdam
• Tel.: 020 572 17 21
• Open the 1st Wednesday and the 3rd Sunday of the month 12-4pm
• Entry charge • Service on Sunday 3pm

A church financed by a lottery

Surprisingly, the Vondel church was "A church actually built after the road in which it had already been constructed. Although it was the first time in several centuries that a new Catholic church could be built without being limited for space by adjacent be seen from all sides, the space available, an oval shaped section in the middle of the street, had to be taken into account nevertheless. As a result, the outlines of this Neo Gothic church followed this oval form to avoid losing space.

Construction began in 1872, but soon came to a halt due to a lack of funds. A lottery was organized and a number of well known people bought lots: Queen Sophie, the Pope and even the French architect Viollet le Duc, who was also Cuypers' master. Thanks to this financing, Pierre Cuypers was able to complete the construction of the church in 1880. Till 1977, it was used for catholic services and named after the "Sacred Heart of Jesus". Nowadays, the venue is rented for private events, for concerts and most recently services are held on Sundays.

TO SEE NEARBY

A PICASSO STATUE IN THE VONDELPARK

The Picasso statue called The Fish, also known as the cut-out shape, has been in the park since 1965. In that year, to celebrate the park's centenary, a sculpture exhibition was organised. At the end of the event, Pablo Picasso made a gift of this statue to the Vondelpark.

MAKE LOVE LEGALLY IN THE VONDELPARK

In Dutch, "to cruise" has nothing to do with sailing off on a luxury boat. It simply means to have sex in a public place. This practice became so established in the Vondelpark that the town council, faced with the situation, preferred to establish some rules.

They decided to authorize such outdoor activity under certain conditions: respect the authorized hours, stay away from playground areas and refrain when there are children in the park. "Doing it in the park, doing it after dark" became the slogan.

Leaving refuse, such as condoms, is forbidden, as are prostitution and exhibitionism.

According to a recent enquiry into nuisances in the Vondelpark, it appears that walkers with unleashed dogs are considered more troublesome than people engaged in open-air sex.

The municipality is going to be much more severe in regard to unleashed dogs!

THE ART NOUVEAU CERAMICS OF THE ATLAS HOTEL ⑯

Hôtel Atlas
• Van Eeghenstraat 64, 1071GK Amsterdam

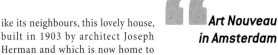

*Art Nouveau
in Amsterdam*

Like its neighbours, this lovely house, built in 1903 by architect Joseph Herman and which is now home to the Atlas Hotel, displays some splendid Art Nouveau ceramic decoration.

Don't miss taking a look not only from the street side (Van Eeghenstraat and Jacob Obrechtstraat), but also from the park side, especially at night when the ceramics are lit.

The ceramics of the villa at No 66 were created by Bert Nienhuis and depict exotic themes, like yellow nasturtiums, symbol of the East Indies, and marabou storks surrounded by water lilies.

On the left-hand panel is the name Lotus, the factory where the ceramics were produced and where Nienhuis worked as a decorator.

On the side, there are two other lovely panels depicting a peacock, also surrounded by water lilies, and the figure of a woman.

On the neighbouring house, at No 64, four oriental portraits can also be seen. Finally, the less well-preserved ceramics at No 62 represent floral motifs composed of exotic violet flowers.

The house at Nos 66-68 Van Eeghenstraat was the residence of Henriette Roland Holst (1869-1952), poetess and left-wing politician (see page 191). The house is the incarnation of the utopian Marxism she expressed in her poetry and political and literary essays.

Ceramic workmanship arrived in Amsterdam via Italian immigrants established in Rotterdam, who in turn had learned from the Moors. The Dutch style developed bit by bit, polychrome motifs giving way to a central design element, either a portrait or an animal, surrounded by geometrical motifs. The use of the colour blue only started at the beginning of the 17th century, following the introduction of blue porcelain from China. Dutch potters did not succeed in mastering the art of making porcelain, but nevertheless they followed the craze for this new style by producing blue monochrome pottery, which found a ready market amongst the wealthy middle classes who used it for embellishing their interiors. But over the centuries, the use of ceramics declined and it was only the arrival of Art Nouveau style that revived the popularity of this decorative material. Today, only three 17th-century factories survive in The Netherlands and continue to produce ceramics, at Makkum, Utrecht and Delft.

TO SEE NEARBY

THE GYPSY "HELL AND FIRE" MONUMENT

On the Museumplein, in front of the U.S. Consulate, stands an interesting monument in homage to Gypsies, sculpted by Helen Levano in the 1960s. It is the first monument in the world devoted to the Gypsy people. It represents a man, woman and child fleeing from a raging fire. Here, the fire represents the hell to which millions of Gypsies were sent during the Second World War. On the base is inscribed the following text "Putrav lesko drom angle leste te na inkrav lemai but palpale mura brigasa", meaning "Build their way to the new life open for them and deliver them from the bonds of sorrow".

Every year, on 1 August, there is a gathering to commemorate the night of 31 July - 1 August 1944, when more than 5000 gypsies were simultaneously gassed in the Auschwitz-Birkenau concentration camp.

THE RUINS IN THE GARDENS OF THE RIJKSMUSEUM
• Free entry, Tuesday to Saturday from 10am-5pm,
Sunday and holidays from 1pm-5pm

In 1890, the garden of the Rijksmuseum was embellished with fragments from buildings destined to disappear from various places in The Netherlands as a result of street widening. Thus was created a permanent exhibition of five centuries of Dutch architecture, ranging from the Gothic columns of the little church or "Kleine Kerk" of Edam to the 18th-century town gates of Groningen and Deventer, for example. On the Jan Luykenstraat side of the garden is a sort of patchwork jumble of fragments from monumental constructions that had to be demolished in the 19th century. Here, one can admire pilasters, lions' heads, festoons and façade stones.

THE TOILETS OF THE COBRA CAFÉ
Hobbemastraat 18, 1071ZB Amsterdam

In the basement toilets of the Cobra Café, the doors are made of a type of transparent glass which only becomes opaque when the doors are locked. Those who forget to do so - and it does happen - are somewhat startled to see customers waiting their turn watching them curiously.

A SWIMMING POOL ON A FORMER BIKE TRACK

The building that houses the "Zuiderbad" swimming pool (or south pool), on the corner of Hobbemastraat and Hobbemakade, was built in 1897 by the architect Jonas Igenhol for a prominent bicycle importer. Riding the 'Grand Bi' bicycles that were so popular at the time required lessons. The largest covered bike track in The Netherlands was located here.

The walls were even protected with mattresses so that elegant ladies who were rigged out in long dresses and high-necked blouses could crash gently if they didn't brake in time. When the bicycling school went bankrupt in 1912, a swimming pool was installed in the building.

As it hadn't been conceived for such a use, the pool, holding 700,000 cubic metres of water, was built above ground. Swimmers must climb steep steps to enter the water.

SHOEBALOO

Pieter Cornelisz. Hooftstraat 80, 1071CB Amsterdam
- Tel.: 020 671 22 10
- Open Tuesday to Saturday 10am to 6pm, Sunday 12 to 6pm, and Thursday evening to 9pm

A futuristic ambiance for luxurious shoes

The Shoebaloo luxury shoe shop is as well-known for its avant-garde interior as for the brands of designer shoes that it offers. A visit to this shop is a must for those who like futuristic surroundings.

The highly design-oriented interior of this shop was created by the architects Roberto Meyer and Jeroen van Schooten. This unusual duo (a Colombian and a Dutchman) set up their practice in 1984 and are particularly well known for their creation of the headquarters of the ING bank, beside the southern ring-road, also called familiarly 'the liner' or 'the shoe'.

Although located in a 19th-century building, this boutique contrasts with the other shops in this fashionable street. Unlike traditional shop-fronts, Shoebaloo has no window facing the street but has mirrored doors that reflect the street and the passers-by. The strangeness of this reflective façade entices shoppers to stop and look. The doors then open onto a high-tech interior reminiscent of a spaceship.

The rectangular interior space is composed of pigeonholes in translucent white polyacrylic, lit from behind by more than 500 fluorescent tubes. There is a system to enable the colour tone of these tubes to be varied, so as to constantly change the atmosphere.

The floor and the low ceiling are linked to the ranges of pigeonholes by a rounded cornice, giving the impression of a bubble. The mirrors at the end of the shop are positioned in such a way that it is very difficult to estimate the real dimensions of the place, which seems a lot bigger than its fifty square metres.

Display units and egg-shaped designer seating complete this quite sci-fi atmosphere.

THE OLD SOUTH DISTRICT POLICE STATION ㉑

Politiebureau
Koninginneweg 29-31, 1071HZ Amsterdam

> *The old tramway horse stables*

The Old South district police station is located in a very attractive building that, in the days of horse-drawn trams, served as the terminus of the Tram 2 line. Architect Adolf Van Gendt built it in 1893, in the style of a small town hall.

The two large openings have been retained. They were built particularly high, one for access by the tramcars to their garage, the other for the passage, to and from their stalls, of the horses that pulled them. Up to 81 horses could be held in these stables, where they were groomed and fed. The tramcars were cleaned here, too. At the time, the city did not extend beyond the Sophialaan, so the tram naturally stopped here, the garage being the end of the line. Beyond, there were only marshes. At the beginning of the 20th century, the tramways were electrified. The stables were not needed anymore but the terminus remained at this location until 1948, when the tracks were extended. It was natural to find another use for the building itself and in 1933 it became a station for the mounted police, the horses occupying one side, the policemen the other.

Today, windows have replaced the large doors, but the police station is still there.

TO SEE NEARBY

THE KONINGSLAAN PALM TREE ㉒
Koningslaan 16, 1075AC Amsterdam

Because the Dutch climate is often very rigorous, only a few rare exotic plants are to be found in Amsterdam. As Koningslaan is rather wide and the buildings fairly low, though, the south side gets plenty of sunshine and next to the road at No 16 stands a very fine Chinese palm tree which can withstand temperatures as low as -15°C.

THE LAIRESSE PHARMACY ㉓

Lairesse Apotheek, De Lairessestraat 40, 1071PB Amsterdam
• Tel.: 020 662 10 22
• Open Monday to Friday 8:30am to 6pm, and Saturday 10am to 5pm

A designer pharmacy

While the Lairesse pharmacy does sell conventional pharmaceutical products, it particularly specialises in natural and homeopathic medicines. Designed in 2004 by Rob Wagemans of the Concrete studio, its concept was to encourage well-being and serenity. Its particularly innovative design is worth a look.

By transforming a small bank branch into a pharmacy, Marjan Terpstra wanted to get away from the atmosphere of the medical world, and provide instead a feeling of harmony between the natural and the synthetic. Upon entering, one is welcomed first by glass cases representing the Mendeleïev tables of the elements. The wide entrance provides access into a round room where the light is filtered and the restful green tones of shop fittings emphasize calm and quiet. More than 500 green Plexiglass drawers line the walls from floor to ceiling. A large photo of gingko leaves covers the floor and one can sit on a curved leather bench after placing one's order at the counter, which is supported by a large tree trunk.

TO SEE NEARBY

THE DUTCH MARIONETTE THEATRE ㉔
Nederlands Marionettentheater, Jacob Obrechtstraat 28,
1071KG Amsterdam • Entry charge

The "Nederlands Marionettentheater" puppeteer group was founded in 1923 by Bert Brugman. His great-grandson, Jonas van Tol, keeps up the tradition. Since 2002, the entertaining shows have taken place in a small room near the Obrechtkerk church. It can be accessed by going through the little door to the right of the church and walking through to the back of the narrow garden alongside the right-hand side of the church.

THE OPEN-AIR SCHOOL

1e Openluchtschool voor het Gezonde Kind
Cliostraat 36-40, 1077KJ Amsterdam

**Learn in
the open air**

The open-air school (Openluchtschool) is worth a visit for its interesting architecture. Built in 1930 by the architect Johannes Duiker, it is hidden in the middle of a courtyard behind Cliostraat, part of H. Berlage's Nieuw Zuid construction plan. It is a fine example of the "Nieuwe Bouwen" ("New Construction") of the 1920s to the 1940s.

Johannes Duiker is one of the main figures of Netherlands functional architecture during the inter-war years. Influenced by Frank Lloyd Wright and Le Corbusier, he extolled the concept of an avant-garde architecture for a utopian society, which left its mark on Dutch architecture.

This spirit can also be found in the creations of Aldo van Eyck (see page 239). While the open-air school was designed as a functional building, the accent was placed on the idea that architecture can contribute to hygiene, seen as a necessary condition for the well-being of the body. For Duiker, the overall architecture had as much influence as the methods of teaching on the success of the school, where the development of the mind cannot be achieved without the development of the body.

The form of the building, inspired by transatlantic liners, which ensures lots of light and air, is of a remarkable form: a half-open cube, with straight lines and surfaces and no nooks and crannies for dust and mites. The main building has a classroom and a gymnasium on the ground floor. Each floor above has two south-facing classrooms with an additional space to hold classes in the open air. The roof terrace also provides an opportunity for pupils to take classes out of doors.

Utilitarianism in architecture is a constant theme of this movement. Nevertheless, while the Hilversum Sanatorium, built by Duiker in 1925, was, of course, designed for the ill, the open-air school was the first of its kind to accommodate children in good health, hence its name "Openluchtschool voor het Gezonde Kind" ("Open-Air School for the Child in Good Health"). Today, this building, classed as a Historical Monument, still houses the Eerste Openluchtschool.

THE COMMEMORATIVE MEMORIAL OF THE NETHERLANDS INDIES

❷❻

Monument Indië Nederland
Olympiaplein, 1077CJ Amsterdam

> *One of the rare symbols of the colonial period*

This impressive monument commemorating The Netherlands Indies is one of the rare symbols of The Netherlands colonial period. The fact that its name has been changed gives a good indication of how the Dutch society's attitude towards colonialism has evolved.

Present-day Indonesia was discovered in 1596 by Houtman, a future V.O.C. captain (see page 50).

Commerce developed quickly through the port of Bantam, and then through Batavia (now Jakarta), which was taken from the English in 1619 by Governor-General Jan Pietersz. Coen.

When the V.O.C. went bankrupt, the Dutch government took over its debts and its possessions. The governor-general there, J. van den Bosch, used his experience in the West Indies to introduce the cultivation of sugar cane using slave labour. As this new form of colonisation proved very profitable, a special army, the KNIL (Koninlijk Nederlands-Indisch Leger - the Royal Army of The Netherlands Indies) was set up in 1830 to gain possession of the whole archipelago. This involved considerable violence, particularly during the Atjeh War in Sumatra (1873-1903), where General J. B. van Heutsz, then commander of the KNIL, won renown for his peace-making efforts.

In 1904, he became governor-general of the entire Netherlands Indies and finalised the frontiers of the country. He died in Switzerland in 1924. Three years after his death he was laid to rest in Amsterdam, in the East cemetery. As this proved less expensive than expected, the remainder of the money was used to erect a monument in his honour. Because of the ambivalent attitude in The Netherlands towards colonisation, the creation of a monument to van Heutsz in Amsterdam aroused violent protests on the part of Communists and Social Democrats. Nevertheless, the structure by Frits van Hall was inaugurated on 15 June 1935 by Queen Wilhelmina, in the presence of Princess Juliana and Prime Minister Colijn.

This monument comprises a commemorative column 18.7m high. On the front is an allegory of Justice: a woman, flanked by two lions, holding a roll of laws.

Through the decades, this monument remained the centre of numerous controversies, the actions of the KNIL having finally come to be regarded as war crimes. In 2004, when the town renovated the monument, it was renamed the "Monument Indië-Nederland" (Netherlands Indies Monument).

All allusion to van Heutsz has disappeared, except for a plaque bearing his portrait.

THE TRAMWAY MUSEUM

Electrische Museumtramlijn Amsterdam, Terminus: Haarlemmermeerstation,
Amstelveenseweg 264, 1075XV Amsterdam
• Sundays from Easter to the end of October 11am to 5:30pm,
details on www.museumtramlijn.org
• Cash needed to pay the fare

The oldest tramway in Amsterdam

Here is something dedicated to those with nostalgia for the past. Tramcars dating from 1904 to 1954 and from different large European cities have been restored and are now driven by volunteers. They travel from the Haarlemmermeer station towards the south of Amsterdam, in a rustic atmosphere, for a return journey lasting about an hour and fifteen minutes.

One can hop onto the tram at any stop, although it is strongly recommended to include the Haarlemmermeer station, which has been preserved in its original character. If you arrive there early, or indeed end your ride there, you can enjoy its attractive terrace in a quiet setting beside the line, where one or two historic trams can be seen. Each car comes from a different town and dates from a different era. The interiors, generally fitted with wooden seats, are decorated with a variety of period advertisements. The tinkle of the bell and the noise of the motor combine to create a unique atmosphere, as do the level crossing signals and the energetic efforts of the controller to stop the traffic with his red flag.

The route passes first behind the Olympic stadium, and then past the ING bank building, continuing along the charming Schinkel port, and then alongside the Amsterdam woods. After that, one passes the little gardens and vegetable plots of a residential area. Take a look at the old Amstelveen station, converted into an antique shop.

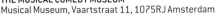

TO SEE NEARBY

THE MUSICAL COMEDY MUSEUM

Musical Museum, Vaartstraat 11, 1075RJ Amsterdam
• Tel.: 020 664 10 78 • Visit by appointment only

This little musical comedy museum was founded by Frans and Thea Gankema after their son-in-law Marco Vermie introduced them to this world of song and stage. He had great success on the European musical scene and this museum traces his performances, notably in Cats. On display are costumes, tickets, programmes, backstage access and more.

THE FORMER ORPHANS' HOUSES   ㉙
IJsbaanpad 3, 1076CV Amsterdam

**An
interpretation
of an African village
by architect
Aldo Van Eyck**

The orphans' houses, used as such from 1960 to 1991, are a striking architectural achievement by Aldo van Eyck. As a modern interpretation of a traditional African village, these buildings are a highly regarded work by this great architect.

Until 1959, the municipal orphanage was located in the town centre (see page 71). From 1955, van Eyck developed the plans for a new orphanage. He took his inspiration from his early 1950's work on schools in Nagele, a new town built on the polders creating a single-storey open plan with interior courtyards and playgrounds.In contrast to the trend at that time, the architect created a type of village with 328 houses, each resembling a square hut, with sides 3.36m long and a convex concrete roof. The architecture reinforced the binary nature of the reception of the 125 children who were treated both as individuals and as a group.These houses are considered to be the first example of Structuralist architecture and have been a source of inspiration in school design for architects worldwide.

STRUCTURALISM

Structuralism is a 20th-century way of thinking which analyses the relationship between the elements of a system and the system itself. In linguistics, for instance, the work of Ferdinand de Saussure does not lay emphasis on the language itself, but on the processes and rules that enable it to generate communication.

The infrastructure of the language, the grammar and the rules, are of more importance than the expressions or common use of the language.

Claude Levi-Strauss' anthropological studies of traditional African and Asian cultures analysed what lay behind people's habitual behaviour, in terms of the underlying structures and relationships of a group.

In the same way, the Structuralist movement in architecture is based on the relationship between the elements, as exemplified by the honeycomb structure inside a beehive.

Structuralism reached its architectural peak in the 1950s and 1960s.

THE PIJP

BOAT-IN PIZZERIA

❶

Pizzeria San Marco, Amstelkade 148a, 1078AW Amsterdam
• Tel.: 020 673 08 84

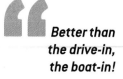

Better than the drive-in, the boat-in!

If you have had the good idea either to own a boat or to rent one (see below), you have the rare privilege of being able to discover the town from a completely different perspective. So, why not take advantage of the opportunity to steer towards the San Marco pizzeria, which has the splendid arrangement of serving you without your having to leave your boat. As you will have guessed, Amsterdam and the owners of the pizzeria have recently invented the clever idea of the 'boat-in', after the henceforth-outdated concept of the 'drive-in'. Forget about passing the order for your Big Mac from behind the steering wheel of your car, in tawdry suburbs, and come here instead to take advantage of all that Amsterdam has to offer.

The pizzeria is situated in one of the four little houses on the bridge over the Amstel canal (Amstelkanaal).

TO HIRE A BOAT IN AMSTERDAM

As in Venice, the best way to see the town is probably still by boat. Clearly we are not suggesting one of the many tourist boats, where the multilingual commentaries will literally put you to sleep. It is just as easy to hire your own boat, even without a permit. The advantage, by comparison with Venice, is, of course, that you won't have to confront numerous gondolas in the narrow canals!

Old-fashioned boats or "salonboten" can be hired by the hour, or the day, with a skipper, and with or without meal service. You can reserve at Lovers (www.lovers.nl) opposite the railway station, The Hilton (www.aquadam.nl) on Apollolaan, or at Cruise with us (www.cruisewithus.nl).

Better still, you can hire an electric boat, without a skipper, from Canal Motorboats (Tel: 020-422 7007).

TO SEE NEARBY

THE BAROMETER OF THE OKURA HOTEL

❷

Ferdinand Bolstraat 333, 1072LH Amsterdam
• Tel.: 020 678 71 11

At a height of 75 metres, the Okura Hotel has the highest barometer in The Netherlands. The upper side of its roof is illuminated by a light. It changes colour according to the atmospheric pressure, offering an observer a good idea of how the weather is evolving. The colour blue indicates fine weather while green signals the arrival of bad weather.

THE GARDENS ON THE WATER
Ruysdaelkade near No 70, 1072AJ Amsterdam

The canals attract nesting water birds that prefer protected sites, under the bridges or on floating masses of debris where nature has intervened in the form of plants.

As they grow, their network of roots in the water attracts small marine creatures and fish that feed on the algae, thus ensuring the water's filtration. Floating gardens develop naturally, whether on an old beam or a collection of debris, like the one near No 70 Ruysdaelkade.

The "Amsterdamse Waterzuivering", a water management organisation, casts a favourable eye on this non-polluting occupation of the bank side, which contributes positively to the purification of the canal water.

These gardens form an ecological ribbon on the town's canals.

THE RIDDLE OF "EGTERS 66"
Jozef Israëlskade 116, 1072SB Amsterdam

At No 116 on the Josef Israël Quay, one can read the inscription "Egters 66". It corresponds to the old house numbering system of this quay, which used to be called the quay of the painters ("Schilderskade"). Dutch writer Gerhard van het Reve (1923-2006) lived here when he was young. The action of his successful book "*de Avonden*" (*The Evenings*) takes place in this house and the famous protagonist is named... Egters!

TO SEE NEARBY

THE HIDDEN STATUE BY ZADKINE

Westeinde 2, 1017ZN Amsterdam

Beside The Netherlands Bank, you will find a bronze statue 4.5 meters high, created by Ossip Zadkine (1880-1967) in 1963. It is called *"De Woning" (The Abode)* and even though it stands on a high plinth, it is often passed unnoticed. Zadkine's first exhibition, in 1923, was at the Gerbrandes gallery in Utrecht. At the time, he was already working on mobile geometric forms. His method of production consisted of pouring plaster onto a shape created from iron wire, sculpting it, then casting it in bronze. In contrast to most sculptors who started from more elaborate forms and then refined them, Zadkine perfected his own method, progressively adding arms, legs or even musical instruments. In 1950, Zadkine produced a series of bronzes comprising two or three separate pieces for the first time. In 1960, he began working on perforated forms, of which "*The Abode*" is a good example.

HOMAGE TO THE VICTIMS OF A SECOND WORLD WAR SHOOTING

1ᵉ Weteringplantsoen, 1017SJ Amsterdam

This fine bronze statue, representing a soldier lying dead with his trumpet in his hand, was produced in 1954 by Gerrit Bolhuis and carries the name *"de gevallen hoornblazer" (The Fallen Trumpeter)*. This statue is an homage to the thirty men who were shot in reprisal for an attempt on the life of a German official on 12 March 1945. It was financed by the Heineken Brewery, which is situated on the other side of the Stadhouderskade.

THE 'BIG BI' AND 'THE PEDERSEN' AT THE FIETS FABRIEK

1e Jacob van Campenstraat 12, 1072BC Amsterdam

In the midst of the innovative creations of Dave Deutsch and Yalçin Cihangir, the Bike Factory, or Fiets Fabriek, is a shop which displays two early cycles. The first, a Big Bi, is an invention of the 1870s that has a very large front wheel turned directly by the pedals and a much smaller rear wheel for stability (see also page 224) — the equivalent of the English 'Penny Farthing' bike. The shop's other attraction is the Pedersen, an 1893 model created by Dursley Pedersen, whose particularity is its construction around a hammock-style leather saddle that connects the front of the bike to the rear.

THE BAZAR RESTAURANT

Albert Cuypstraat 182, 1073BL Amsterdam
• Tel.: 020 675 05 44 • Open Mon-Thurs 11am to midnight;
Fri-Sat 11am to 1am
• Market open daily except Sunday

The Bazar restaurant owes its interest to the extraordinary building which houses it: an enormous building hidden in the middle of the Albert Cuyp market. It was built in 1951 to serve as a Reform Church named Buiten Amstel, but was later converted into a supermarket. It then housed a record shop, and then a baroque bar, before becoming a restaurant serving international cuisine, an offshoot of the well-known Bazar Hotel in Rotterdam.

Albert Cuyp Street is well known for its daily market. Until 1883, this street was called the "Zaagmolensloot", or street of the sawmill ditches. The ditch was filled in and the street took the name of Albert Cuyp, a 17th-century painter from Dordrecht.

THE FORMER ASSCHER DIAMOND WORKS ❾

Diamantslijperij Asscher, Tolstraat 127-129, 1074VJ Amsterdam

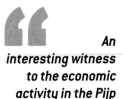

An interesting witness to the economic activity in the Pijp

Joseph Isaac Asscher started a diamond cutting business on the Nieuwe Achtergracht in 1854. At the beginning of the 20th century, the firm still belonged to two of his grandsons, Abraham and Joseph Asscher. The latter was a very talented diamond cutter.

In 1902, he obtained a patent for a new diamond cut of eight facets, which gained the Asscher firm an international reputation.

As a result of the substantial increase in business, architect Gerrit van Arkel was commissioned in 1906 to construct a new building, and, in 1907, the factory moved to the Tolsraat in the Pijp, which was then a new district of Amsterdam.

Built entirely from yellow and red bricks, the building is surprising for its numerous openings, which were provided to ensure the level of light needed for the minute cutting of these precious stones. The crenellations on the roof give it something of the air of a medieval castle.

At the peak of the factory's activity, nearly 750 people cut diamonds here in Tolstraat. Just before the Second World War, there were still 500, but only 15 survived. The Asscher family was also decimated, leaving only ten survivors, among whom were Joop and Louis Asscher. The two men used their experience to start a new business in New York in 1946, which has continued on successfully until today.

The Diamond Quarter ("diamantbuurt") was created around 1930 in the style of the Amsterdam School (see page 270).

As in the "Nieuw Zuid" (New South) district, the streets contain sculptures by Hildo Krop. You can see, for example, a mother suckling her babies, a symbol of the worker's life of the 20th century, on the façade in Diamantstraat.

The streets in this quarter all have names of precious stones: diamonds (Diamantstraat), sapphires (Saffierstraat), rubies (Robijnstraat), topazes (toppaasstraat) and emeralds (Smaragstraat).

Numerous small houses were built in this quarter by architect Leonard van Gendt to house the factory's workers. Examples can be seen at Nos 1-11 Robijnstraat and Nos 1-22 Diamantstraat.

TO SEE NEARBY

THE CONTROVERSIAL ORIGINS OF THE HOUSES WITH THE GOBLINS
Ceintuurbaan 251-255, 1074CZ Amsterdam

Any walker looking upwards to the roof level of these attractive neo-Gothic style houses, designed by architect A.C. Boerma in 1884, can't fail to spot two green and red goblins playing ball. Two explanations have been put forward to explain their presence.

According to the first one, the goblins playing ball are an allusion to the name of the man who ordered the building – Mr. van Ballegooijen, whose name in Dutch means "ball-thrower". The other explanation relates to the Dutch expression "elkar de bal toespellen" (to pass the ball from one to the other). The builder who built these houses in 1884 found himself short of money and had to "pass the ball" to a fellow builder who completed the construction.

THE FORMER CINETOL CINEMA
Public Library, Tolstraat 160, 1074VN Amsterdam
• Tel.: 020 662 31 84
• Open Mon to Wed 2pm to 5:30pm, Fri and Sat 11am to 4pm

In this small hidden street, this very attractive building in the Nieuwe Bouwen style (see page 233) is called "Cinetol", a contraction of Cinema and de Tol. The word "Tol" is an allusion to "Tolhek", the customs tollgate that was situated there till 1896, when the northern part of Nieuwer-Amstel was annexed to Amsterdam. This building was certainly used as a cinema during the Second World War, although it was originally conceived as a temple. In 1926, a group of rich Amsterdammers commissioned the architects Brinkman and van der Vlught to create a theosophical temple. Saved from destruction, it has been used as an annexe of the municipal library since 1985.

THE GABLE STONE OF ST ANDREWS CROSSES
Amsteldijk 67, 1074HZ Amsterdam

The impressive building at No 67 Amsteldijk was built in 1892, in neo-Renaissance style, by the architect R. Kuipers. Above the door is an interesting gable stone representing St Andrews crosses: three side by side and one below. This building used to house the Town Hall of Nieuwer-Amstel, which at the time was a separate village from Amsterdam, and whose coat of arms included the crosses. The northern part of this village was annexed to Amsterdam and the southern part took the name of Amstelveen in 1964.

A FORMER PUMPING STATION
Oud gemaal op de Ruysdaelkade • Ruysdaelkade 2, 1072AG Amsterdam
• Tel.: 020 672 25 25

Ruysdaelkade is situated on the former "Boerenwetering" or "The stream of the farmers", a polder district in the heart of the town. At No 2, behind a brick wall, is an old pumping station. Nowadays, this building is occupied by a cultural association called SKQR that supports cultural projects through advice and finance.

TO SEE NEARBY

THE LAST LITTLE POLDER HOUSE

Rustenburgerstraat 8, 1073GA Amsterdam

The little polder house ("polderhuisje") in the Pijp district is an amusing little worker's house. In the 19th century, this district was part of Nieuwer-Amstel and was in the country, between pastures and the summer residences of rich Amsterdammers.

In 1860, the painter Jan van Bemmel came to live in this district. Given the shortage of housing, and being a good businessman, he had some houses built, using the slogan "een huis van steen, met pannen gedekt" (a stone house with a tiled roof). This little house, built in 1865, is still there and has been entirely renovated by its owner.

THE HISTORY OF THE PIJP

The district extending from the south to the centre was built at the end of the 19th century. Originally it was called "buurt YY" (YY district), referring to the 50th district on the grand urban development plan, where each district was designated by one or two letters (from A to Z then AA to ZZ).

The north part of the Pijp was built in the 1860s and the south part followed thirty years later. The street plan of the north part followed the existing roads and ditches, to which were added three streets crossing between them. The second one, Jacob van Campenstraat, thus joins Gerard Doustraat rather strangely, at an angle. The houses on the corners of these streets are thus pointed, which is why they are called "tartpunten" (points of a tart).

The name Pijp was soon adopted to refer to this district. In Dutch, one of the meanings of "Pijp" is a long, narrow stream. This could be an allusion to the human river formed by the workers of the time as they streamed into the centre to work each morning.

FERDINAND BOL IN THE PIJP

In the north part of the Pijp, all the streets are named after famous 17th-century painters. Ferdinand Bol street owes its name to this Dordrecht painter, a pupil of Rembrandt and Albert Cuyp. The Rijksmuseum holds numerous portraits painted by him. After his marriage to the wealthy widow Anna van Arckel (see page 162, van Loon house), Ferdinand Bol gave up painting at the age of 53. In 1941, baker J.I. de Borst opened a shop in this street. Inspired by the name of the street (Ferdinand Bolstraat), he named his shop "Febo House". He had the idea of selling his products through automatic dispensers. Today, the firm has 60 branches and has been run since 1990 by the son of the founder. This success has become so embedded in Dutch culture that people say "uit de muur eten" (eat from the wall) to refer to buying a croquette or another local speciality at Febos.

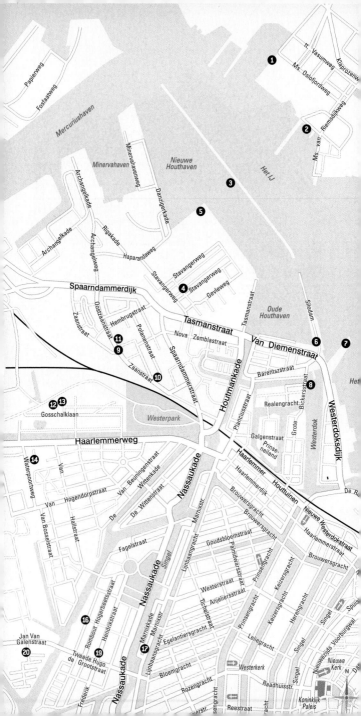

THE NORTHWESTERN ISLES DISTRICT

KRAANSPOOR ❶

Kraanspoor, Oslofjordweg 40, 1033SE Amsterdam,
Formerly Vasumweg 63, 1033 SE Amsterdam

> **A surprising ecological building**

This building is very large: 270m long, with an impressive expanse of glass almost 15m high. It contains nearly 12,000m² of offices. Determinedly modern, it is a reminder of the intensive harbour activity of the northwest part of the port of Amsterdam until the end of the 1970s.

In 1952, the NDSM (Nederlandse Dok en Scheepsbouw Mattschappij, or Dutch Port and Ship Construction Authority) ordered the construction of a rail track, built on an enormous concrete base. On this track, travelling cranes facilitated the loading and unloading of cargoes.

In 1979, the yards were closed and abandoned. Twenty years later, the architects Trude Hooykaas and Julian Wolse, from the firm OTH, transformed this place and created a remarkable building, one of the most energy-efficient in the world.

The façade is composed of double glass panels that can open and close, creating natural air currents and acting as a screen to counteract the greenhouse effect, thus better controlling the internal temperature.

A pump-like system uses the water temperature of the river to cool the building in summer and warm it in winter. Inaugurated in 2008, the building has been used as a model of architecture worldwide.

A small area of the former NDSM yards, beside the maritime district of Amsterdam North, houses a small shipyard devoted to the restoration and maintenance of antique and collectable boats.

TO SEE NEARBY

THE HARBOUR CANTEEN ❷

- Café-restaurant IJ-Kantine, M.T. Ordinaweg 15-17, 1033RE Amsterdam
- Open Monday to Friday from 7am, week-end from 9am
- Tel.: 020 633 71 62. Accessible by ferry N.D.S.M. from Central Station

This building, constructed in 1957, served as a canteen for the workers in the NDSM yards until 1979. After the closure of the yards, the old buildings were squatted by homeless people and artists. The canteen became the centre of the unemployed dockers association. During the district's renovation, most of the buildings acquired a cultural dimension, particularly the MTV Benelux centre. The canteen reclaimed its former function and has become a very pleasant restaurant with a lovely view over the harbour.

THE R.E.M. ISLAND ❸

Haparandadam 45-II 1013AK Amsterdam
• Tel.: 020 688 55 01 • Open Tuesday to Sunday
8pm-1am, Friday and Saturday till 3am

A former illegal broadcasting platform

This restaurant located on a platform on the IJ, offering a unique view on the river, has a rather surprising story, illustrating the courage and creativity for more freedom in the 1960s. Till then, the Netherlands offered only one official TV station, shared by 6 broadcasting private associations who distributed the time slots. Advertising was forbidden. To bypass this limitation, one of them decided to broadcast offshore, like radio ships were already doing. They had a platform made in the shipyards of Cork in Ireland and installed on the seabed, 9 km away from the coast of Noordwijk. The Advertising Operating Company (Reclame Exploitatie Maatschappij or R.E.M.) was created in 1963 and financed through a successful subscription of 350.000 shares. The broadcasting started on August 15th 1964. The channel became quickly popular with programs such as Rin Tin Tin and Hitchcock movies. The reaction of the government was pretty quick: 4 months later, a new law extended the territorial waters to 11.5km. As the platform could not be moved, the equipment of the R.E.M. was confiscated. A year later, the broadcasting resumed officially in Hilversum under the name TROS (Televisie Radio Omroep Stichting), which also mean "hawser" in Dutch, as a reminder of the past. The platform was used as a monitoring centre to measure wave height, water temperature and salt concentration in the North Sea. This activity stopped in 2004. In the absence of a buyer, the dismantling of the platform started in a shipyard in Vlaardingen, till the Housing Corporation "De Key" decided to buy the platform and turn it into a new place on the river IJ. On the second floor, you can now enjoy a nice dinner.

TO SEE NEARBY

PREFABS FOR STUDENTS ❹

Stavangerweg 50-877
• Gevleweg 20-94 • Oslofjordweg 557, Amsterdam

715 prefabricated lodgings have been installed on the industrial wastelands of the port, on the former N.D.S.M. location. Designed by the HVDN architects, the staked containers were conceived as a temporary village to meet the shortage of student housing. The rather dull design has been livened up by different-sized windows of harmonious proportions and the use of Plexiglas panels in bright colours.

PONT 13 Haparandadam 50, 1013AK Amsterdam ❺

• Open Monday to Saturday from 1pm, Sunday from 12pm
• Tel.: 020 770 27 22

Pont 13" stands for Ferry 13, as it was used to cross the river IJ till 1990. About to be sold as scrap, the ferry was saved by René Langendijk and turned into a cozy restaurant.

THE KORTHALS ALTES GRAIN SILOS ❻

Silodam 109-253, 1013AS Amsterdam

> *Silos for a military defence system*

Situated in the port district, one could easily imagine that the massive Korthals Altes grain silo is a remnant of Dutch commercial prosperity. In fact, it's an example of the town's defence policy instituted at the end of the 19th century.

This new defence policy was drafted in 1874. Its principle was to make a clean sweep of earlier fortifications and to construct a coherent new system based on concentric lines of defence. The shortest, innermost circle was the line around the town itself (the 'Stelling van Amsterdam'), comprising an ingenious system of 42 forts, plus dikes, barrages and locks to enable the surroundings of the town to be flooded in two days.

It was designed not only to isolate the city from the enemy, but also to enable it to withstand a siege. J. Ph. Korthals Altes (1827-1904), a municipal councillor, had a grain and flour silo built between 1886 and 1889 by architects Jacob Klinkhamer (1854-1929) and Adolf Van Gendt (1835-1901). The port activity of Amsterdam was, at that time, being moved westwards, as access to the sea had been facilitated by the opening of the North Sea Canal in 1876. For this reason, it was natural to locate the silo on the west side of the port.

The grain silo is an impressive building that is 104.55m long, 20.45m wide and 26.6m high.

Built entirely of bricks, it combines the majesty of a castle with the enclosed character of a fort. It could hold 16,730 tonnes of grain in 120 containers.

In 1987, the silo was converted into dwellings by architect A. van Stigt. While the silhouette of the building has been preserved, its solidity has been lightened by the insertion of large vertical windows. In 1952, a second grain silo was added to increase the storage capacity. It too was converted and has been inhabited since 1999.

The Stelling van Amsterdam is one of the six monuments in The Netherlands classed as world heritage sites by UNESCO.

TO SEE NEARBY

THE STENEN HOOFD BEACH ❼
Westerdoksdijk 40,
1013AE Amsterdam

In the summer, don't miss taking a walk on the Stenen Hoofd jetty in the middle of the Westerdoksdijk. Specially designed in 1905 to receive the largest ships, it has been in disuse since 1968 and is transformed into a beach in the high season.

THE CAPTAINS' HOUSES OF THE REALENEILAND

The three artificial islands of Prinseneiland, Bickerseiland and Realeneiland were constructed between 1610 and 1615 to enlarge the area of the commercial harbour. Today, only a few vestiges remain of the considerable economic activity of the yards and docks of the 17th century. Nevertheless, do take the time to walk along the Zandhoek Quay where there are 13 pretty houses. At the time when this quay was actually beside the river IJ, they provided lodgings for ship captains between their long voyages.

One of the most interesting houses, now a café-restaurant, is at No 14 at the end of the quay, and was built by Reynier Reale in 1624. His name is reflected in the gable stone representing a "gouden reale",

 a Spanish gold coin of the 16th century. In the middle of the coin is a portrait of Charles V. On the edge of the coin, one can read "CAROLUS D.G. ROM.IMPE.Z.HISP.REX" ("Charles by the grace of God, Emperor of Rome and King of Spain"), words whose significance relates to the binding decree by Charles V at Brussels in 1549, which made the United Provinces a separate state within the Germanic Roman Empire. This "real" refers to the name of the owner.

At No 12 is a fine gable stone, which has been restored, representing a ship ready to unload its cargo via the gangplank. The text beneath the illustration reads "Noyt Gedogt" or "One would never have expected it".

At No 11, one can see another fine maritime-themed gable stone called "in 't anker" (the anchor). Surprisingly, this gable stone was only installed in 1967 when the house was renovated.

The well-known photographer Jacob Olie (1834 - 1905) was born at No 10, in the house bought by his great-grandfather in 1792.

The house at No 7 was built by Captain Hoogeboom, whose name is visible on the fanlight above the door. This name means "tall tree" in Dutch. The house at No 6 was built in 1657 by Claes Jansz. Essendelft and adorned with a gable stone depicting a horse drinking, taken from the family's coat of arms.

The house at No 4, built in 1658, has several gable stones on biblical themes (see page 82), including St Peter with a fish in one hand and the keys of Paradise in the other, Noah's ark with two birds attending the animals entering via the gangplank and, finally, a representation of John the Baptist with the paralysed man at his feet.

 Dating from 1660, the stone at No 3 depicts the "Eendracht", the Dutch lion, with a sword and a quiver, which is thought to represent the alliance of the seven United Provinces of the Low Countries against Philip the Second of Spain.

Don't miss the chance to admire this row of houses from the end of the quay. It provides an excellent perspective of various types of gables: step gable, neck gable and simple cornice types.

The district took the name "Gouden Real" after the success of the book of the same name. Written in 1940 by Jan Mens, who lived in this district, the novel takes place here.

A heritage of the West Indies Company's trading, tobacco has long been associated with this island, where the British American Tobacco Company's warehouses were located. In 1987, the factory here was replaced by new housing and the square was renamed "Jan Mens."

A WALK THROUGH THE OLD DOCKS AND SHIPYARDS

Since the 1880's, the old dock district has been separated from the town centre by the railway line between Central Station and Haarlem. Although it remains close to the town centre, it is not on the traditional walking routes. The names of the streets tell us much about its 17th and 18th century history centred on the shipyards and fish merchants.

While the isles were developed in the early 17th century, the timber docks, or "Houthaven", are a part of the port which was developed in 1876, at the time when the North Sea Canal was dug and the naval yards moved from the east to the west of the harbour. Starting in the northern part of this district you encounter **Silodam**, the quay of silos.

Continuing, you come to **Bokkinghangenstraat** (the street of the herring smokeries) where the fish that was to be smoked was spread out. You then arrive at **Zoutkeetsgracht** (the salt bins canal) along which stood containers in which fish was salted. When this market declined, these installations were used for storing tar.

The attractive white drawbridge nearby, dating from the 17th century, has had various names over the course of time: Petamayenbrug, Bokkinghangenbrug and Zoutkeetsbrug. It leads to the **Zandhoek** (the sand corner), where the market for sand used for ships' ballast used to be.

Perpendicular is **Taanstraat**. Here, in the 17th century, ships' sails and fishing nets were tanned, by boiling them in vats in an oak-bark mixture, in order to protect them against heat and mildew. The mixture's colour gave the sails that attractive brown that is still known today. Turn left to return to the Realengracht canal and **Vierwindendwarsstraat** (street of the four winds).

Cross the **Drieharingenbrug** (bridge of the three herrings). This manually operated drawbridge lowers when you walk onto the moving section. Spanning the Realengracht, it links Prinseneiland with Realeneiland and owes its name to the house called The Three Herrings at the corner of Vierwindendwarsstraat (No 1), recognisable by the gable stone with three fish above the door.

Proceed along the island of Prinseneiland, where a tour of the warehouses is not to be missed (see following page), and continue as far as the **Galgenstraat** intersection. In the 17th and 18th centuries, from this street, there was a very clear view of the "galgen", or scaffolds, on the other side of the River IJ, on the semi-island where the Volewijck district is now situated.

Continuing to the right, you arrive at the **Nieuwe Teertuinen**. On this spot were the tarring yards for boats. Tar (teer) and pitch were used in the old days to make boats waterproof.

As this activity gave off bad smells and could set off fires, it had been moved from the centre of Amsterdam, further way from inhabited areas.

Close by, as you return, are **Eerste** and **Tweede** (First and Second) **Breeuwerstraat**; the word "breeuwen" means the joints between the planks of the hull of a boat.

Finally, going back onto the 'mainland' you arrive on the **Haarlemmer Houttuinen** (the Haarlem timber yards), where wood was cut into planks and prepared for the shipbuilding yards. In 1632, a canal from Haarlem, called the Haarlemmertrekvaart, was specifically dug to facilitate the transport of timber.

THE OLDEST SHIPYARD IN THE NETHERLANDS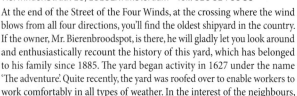

❽

Vierwindenstraat 10, 1013 LA Amsterdam • Tel.: 020 624 50 99

At the end of the Street of the Four Winds, at the crossing where the wind blows from all four directions, you'll find the oldest shipyard in the country. If the owner, Mr. Bierenbroodspot, is there, he will gladly let you look around and enthusiastically recount the history of this yard, which has belonged to his family since 1885. The yard began activity in 1627 under the name 'The adventure'. Quite recently, the yard was roofed over to enable workers to work comfortably in all types of weather. In the interest of the neighbours, work is only permitted from 8:30am to 4pm.

The warehouse district of Prinseneiland has welcomed some well-known people. The painter and photographer **George Hendrik Breitner** (1857-1923), known for his Manet-style realism, worked and lived at No 24b Prinseneiland until 1914.

Today, the painter **Urban Larson** lives in the same house.

At Nos 49-51 live **Ans Markus** and her companion Wybe Tuinman. This contemporary painter is well known for her canvases, particularly portraits of the Queen.

On this building, look for the gable stones created by Hans 't Mannetje in the early 1990s and particularly the amusing composition of the lower one.

It represents Wybe's motorboat, with above it the inscription of Mark 4:14, an allusion to the family name of Ans, and the phrase from the Evangelist of St Mark: "he who sows, sows the word". Beneath, one can read "Laat velen welvaren" (make us prosper).

The exhibition gallery is nearby, at No 14a (visit on request: call 020 620 50 96).

THE WAREHOUSES OF THE ISLE OF PRINCES

Prinseneiland (The Isle of Princes) is one of three isles of Amsterdam, together with Bickerseiland and Realeneiland, which began to be artificially created in 1624.

While the last two bear the names of the great merchant families in the Caribbean trade (Jan Bicker and Reynier Reael), who owned them, the third probably owes its name to the building called The Three Princes (Willem, Mauritz and Fredrik Hendrik), which, at the beginning of the 17th century, was one of the best known locations in the district, but was demolished around 1800.

A whole group of small and large industries and, above all, warehouses were installed on this isle. Of the city's 800 warehouses, 100 were located here, hence its name "voorraadschuren" or commodities stores.

Up until the Second World War, this industrial area was completely deserted outside working hours. In a remarkable change of destiny, these warehouses have been rehabilitated and are now luxury apartments. From being an area to which undesirable industries were consigned, Prinseneiland has become a fashionable neighbourhood, with its village atmosphere, close to the heart of the town.

At Nos 65 to 73 is a series of identical warehouses with spout gables (see page 177 for explanations), with the names "Schelvis" (haddock), "d' Korenbeurs" (the grain store), "D' Gouden Kop" (the golden head), "Broek in Waterland" (from the name of a village close to Amsterdam), and "Mars" (the god of war). All these names have links with the glorious naval past of The Netherlands.

At Nos 111-113, a gable stone reads "The White Pelican". The white pelican is the symbol of Christ and more generally of the spirit of sacrifice. In olden times, people believed that baby pelicans drank their mother's blood. In reality, she loses her feathers after having produced her brood, so her skin appears red.

At numbers 475-545, note a fine series of warehouses built in 1650 and bearing interesting names. The first is called "Klaphout" (cleft timber). Here, oak that had been split into staves ready for use by barrel makers was stocked. The second is called "Korenschuur" (The cereal barn). The third is called "teerton" (tar cask), and the last "De Grote Windhond" (the great greyhound). On this building are three gable stones: the lower one shows a hunter with his dog, the middle one a greyhound and the top one the date of construction.

THE HET SCHIP WORKERS HOUSING ❾

Het Schip Museum, entry at Spaarndammerplantsoen 140,
1013XT Amsterdam • Entry to the apartment, Hembrugstraat 283
• Tel.: 020 418 28 85 • Open Tuesday to Sunday 11am to 5pm,
• Guided tour every hour
• Entry charge

> **The School
> of Amsterdam
> at the service
> of worker well-being**

A visit to one of the workers' lodgings in the Het Schip complex allows a glimpse into the lives of workers in the early 20th century, while appreciating the superb decorative elements of the Amsterdam School.

In the context of an urban development plan for this quarter, Michel de Klerk, one of the founders of the Amsterdam School, was commissioned in 1910 to construct 102 workers' lodgings to the west of Amsterdam, as well as a school and a post office. Behind the façades are three-room lodgings, arranged symmetrically to the left and right of the entrance. The first phase of the lodgings was constructed between 1913 and 1915 on the Spaarndammerplantsoen; the homes were destined for workers in the neighbouring harbour area. This complex is called Het Schip (The Ship), as the building has numerous elements that remind one of a ship. The round windows on the corner of Hembrugstraat resemble the portholes of 17th-century sailing boats while the roof is covered with black tiles intended to represent the prow of a ship.

The philosophy of the Amsterdam School is well illustrated in these buildings with their unconventional shapes. Note the whimsical use of bricks, and the shapes of walls, with unique towers, and - very typical of this style - very small windows. Sculptures produced by Hildo Krop break the monotony. Notice, for instance, the pelicans at the corner of Spaarndammerplantsoen and Zaanstraat, the waves on the Oostzanstraat side of the building and, a bit further on, by Nos 37-43, an amusing white mill, an allusion to the workers who left the Zaandam region to work in Amsterdam. Social life was at the heart of the Amsterdam School's philosophy. The complex was built around an existing school that was integrated into the architecture. It can easily be identified by the dark brown colour of the bricks, on the Oostzanstraat. A post office, where the museum is situated, was also part of the project. Note the attention to detail inside, and the presence of a public telephone, in the forefront of progress at that time.

Finally, personal fulfilment was also provided for. Each block of houses shared several small gardens accessed by a central entry, an interior courtyard, a neighbourhood centre and a playground.

TO SEE NEARBY

THE PUBLIC BATHS ❿
Zaanstraat 88, 1013RW Amsterdam

This building, today used as a hammam, housed public baths at the beginning of the century, as workers' houses did not have bathrooms. Pretty mosaics on the façade are an interesting illustration of the past.

THE AMSTERDAM SCHOOL

The artistic movement called the Amsterdam School dates from the beginning of the 20th century. In the spirit of movements like Expressionism and Art Deco, it developed in combination with the architecture of Hendrik Berlage.

The Amsterdam School is characterized by exotic motifs, with much decoration in low-relief and high-relief, as exemplified by numerous works by sculptor Hildo Krop. The School's imaginative use of bricks included alternating horizontal and vertical layers, as well as the use of red and yellow or the creation of unusual round forms where walls were pierced with little openings.

The Stock Exchange, on the Damrak, was the first building designed by Berlage. Opened in 1903, it inaugurated a new stylistic era for several architects who aspired to an ideal. To be noted amongst the most famous are J.M. van der Mey, the Van Gendt brothers, P.L. Kramer and M. de Klerk, who illustrated the mastery of their art on the house of the ship-owners (see page 55).

The perfect harmony between the inside and the outside of buildings is also characteristic of this style. Around 1900, the municipality asked Berlage to produce a town plan for an extension in South Amsterdam. Ready in 1915, Berlage's plan was intended to promote the blossoming of a new classless, orderly society, giving workers access to art and culture through the use of sculptured ornamentation on all the structures near their homes, including bridges.

In the same spirit, he located libraries in the middle of the neighbourhood, reducing the number of windows to a minimum so as to leave space for numerous decorative elements, including low-relief sculptures, on the walls.

Berlage had studied in Switzerland and had been in contact with Baron Haussman in Paris. He copied Haussman's wide main roads and T-junctions. He demanded that all of the South Plan be developed and carried out at the same time, under the supervision of an aesthetic commission and of a silhouette commission that controlled the profiles of the streets, the height of façades and slopes of roofs.

His residential blocks are four stories high, for the most part. The same materials are used throughout, and yet each street is different. Churchilllaan, for example, is characterized by its variety of entrances and doors and its street corners.

The large-scale residential blocks, creatively varied to ensure that each part of the district had its own character, often had a public garden in the centre. Many decorative elements can be seen, including geometric forms such as parabolas and trapezoids, carved into the building materials and used in the construction of the windows.

In the space of 20 years, hundreds of buildings and thousands of dwellings allying unity and diversity, and of very good quality overall, were built.

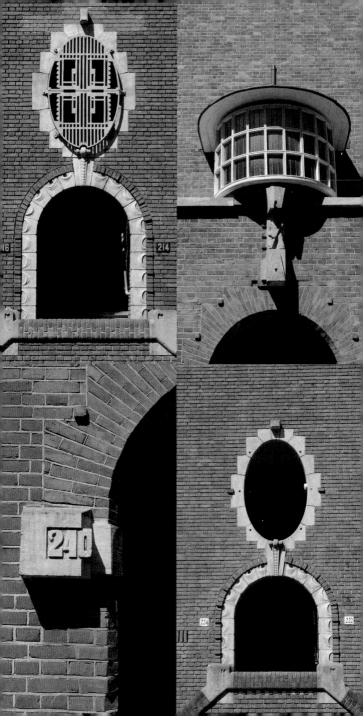

THE AMSTERDAM SCHOOL STREET FURNITURE ⑪

The garden of the "Het Schip" museum café
• Oostzaanstraat 28, 1013WL Amsterdam
• Open from Tuesday to Sunday
from 11am to 5pm

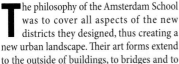

The Amsterdam School "Girobus" letter box

The philosophy of the Amsterdam School was to cover all aspects of the new districts they designed, thus creating a new urban landscape. Their art forms extend to the outside of buildings, to bridges and to street furniture. In the garden of the "Het Schip" museum café, you can see various examples of their blue Girobus letterboxes. The first Girobus box was produced in 1918 by P. L. Marnette. It takes the form of a vertical cylinder mounted on the ground with a fluted design. On the upper half, you can read the words "Gemeentelijk Girokantoor" (municipal post-office), written in a letter type typical of this style, together with the arms of the town of Amsterdam. With the geographical expansion of the town, the need for letterboxes grew and this first model was replaced by a smaller form, designed by architect A. Kurvers. The iron model that he produced in 1926 was nicknamed "the helmet" because of the shape of the upper section. You can see an example in the Zaanstraat Street. One can also see an example of the public urinals called "De Krul" (the curl) because of their S form, conceived by architect Jo van der Mey. Twenty-eight examples of these urinals still exist in the town, notably close to the "Magere brug" bridge, on the Stadhouderskade, on the Prinsengracht and on the Keizersgracht. You can also see examples of lampposts and wrought iron waste bins with yellow trim.

URINALS IN THE AMSTERDAM SCHOOL STYLE

Other urinals in the Amsterdam School style are still in use. In particular, look for one designed by sculptor Hildo Krop, situated on the Oudezijdsvoorburgwal opposite No 193, close to the The Grand hotel. It was built of concrete, stone and brick and is now classed as a historical monument.

THE HISTORY OF THE "POSTGIRO" POSTAL ORDERS

The Girobus letterbox was designed in 1917 to receive the blue envelopes containing a postal order being sent to the tax service or a letter being sent to the municipal services. It was not necessary to stamp these letters, which were handled directly by the municipal service Gemeente Giro. This service resulted from the 1917 merger of the Royal Savings Bank (Rijkspostspaarbank) dating from 1881, with the public Post and Telephone Service PTT. Around 1920, the Gemeente Giro developed the first system of payment by postal orders and postal cheques. Taken over in 1979 by the National Post Giro Service, it later merged in 1989 with NMB (Nederlandse Middenstand Bank) and finally, on 9 February 2009, it became part of the ING Bank.

THE WEST GASWORKS ⓬

Westergasfabriek, Polonceaukade 23, 1014DA Amsterdam
- Tel.: 020 586 07 10
- Park open 24hrs each day

Very interesting neo-Renaissance style industrial buildings

The West Gasworks is a group of 19th-century industrial buildings that have been saved from demolition and converted into a leisure and culture centre. The whole complex has retained a certain charm, a testimony to the Neo-Renaissance style of its architect, Isaac Gosschalk.

Close by, American landscape architect Katheryn Gustafson, who was responsible for the Parc de la Villette in Paris, has created a lively undulating park that is a very attractive place to walk and where water plays a predominant role. The buildings are used regularly for festivals, operas, circuses and private events.

Constructed in 1883 by the British Imperial Continental Gas Company, the West Gasworks was the largest coal-gas production works in Amsterdam at the time. Before the discovery of natural gas in the 1960s at Slochteren, in the north of the country, the gas used for street lighting in the town was produced here.

After having been used as warehouses, then as parking for construction vehicles, the buildings that had not yet been destroyed were classified as monuments in 1989, thus saving them from destruction.

The Park was reopened in 2003, although some buildings are still being restored. Don't miss the "Gas Holder", a great circular gasometer dating from 1903, and the Zuiveringsgebouw, a building for gas scrubbing dating from 1885.

TO SEE NEARBY

THE "KUNSTFABRIEK" ART WORKSHOP ⓭
Polonceaukade 20, 1014DA Amsterdam
- Tel.: 020 488 94 30 • Open Tuesday to Sunday 12-5pm

In this district, the "Kunstfabriek" gallery, which calls itself an art workshop, is run by Jan Peter van Doorn, a former publicity agent, and Bert-Jan van Egteren, a former specialist in contemporary art at Christies.

These two choose pictures and photos, which they then have reproduced to a grand scale in acrylic in China.

The results are stunning.

TO SEE NEARBY

THE AMSTERDAM CAFÉ-RESTAURANT ⓮
Watertorenplein 6, 1051PA Amsterdam • Tel.: 020 682 26 66
• Entry charge • Open 10:30am to midnight, Sat and Sun till 1am

The Amsterdam Café-Restaurant is located in a structure that was built as a pumping station for the Amsterdam water supply. This industrial building has an impressive interior space and interesting relics of its former use, like the rather large old diesel engine.

In 1851, the "NV Duinwater-Maatschappij" (Dunes Water Company) was created to put a revolutionary idea into practice – to bring water freshly filtered by the dunes of Vogelenzang to the inhabitants of Amsterdam.

At first, there was a lack of confidence in this water which was not considered clean, but during the very severe winter of 1853, the normal water supply was cut off since the tanker boats used to transport water became stuck in the frozen river.

The distribution of the water from the dunes was provisionally authorised,

which provided the chance to prove its purity.

The water was pumped through 23 km of pipes to reach the town. At first it was sold by the bucket, near the Haarlemmerpoort, for 1 florin a bucket, but then the installations were extended, so that bit by bit customers were linked to the network.

The works at Vogelenzang soon became inadequate, so this building was constructed in 1897 to increase the distribution capacity.

Behind the works are four large reservoirs, each holding 10,000 cubic metres of water, from which the pipes lead to the town, thus explaining the need for powerful pumps. This station was in use until 1996.

THE PUMPING STATION AT VOGELENZANG ⓯
De Oranjekom Information Centre, 1e Lelyweg 6, 2114BH Vogelenzang
• Tel.: 020 608 75 95 • Open Tuesday to Sunday, 10am to 5pm

The old pumping station of the Vogelenzang water supply pipelines to Amsterdam (Amsterdamse waterleidingduinen), the oldest in The Netherlands, has been restored and is used as a tourist information centre. Situated between Zandvoort and Noordwijk, this is a good starting point for exploring the 3400 hectares of the natural dunes landscape containing a rich variety of flora and fauna.

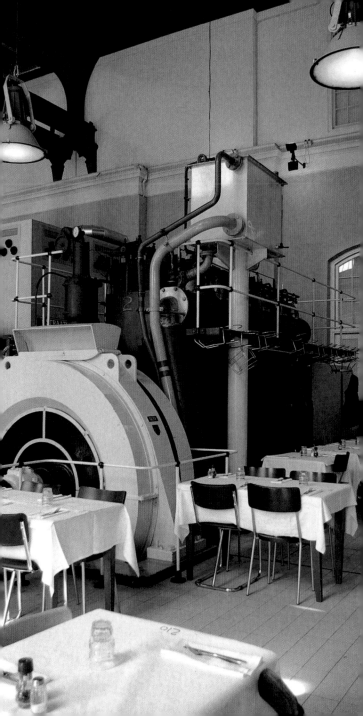

AMSTERDAM'S OTHER SURVIVING MILLS

Molen van Sloten, Akersluis 10, 1066EZ Amsterdam (1847). This mill is still used to keep the nearby polders dry. It is open to the public and attracts numerous tourists.

De Bloem, Haarlemmerweg 465, 1055PK, Amsterdam (1768). This mill was used for milling grain until the early 1950s. It was originally just to the north of the Jordaan, but was moved to make way for houses.

De 1200 Roe, (Roe standing for Roeden, a former measuring unit), Haarlemmerweg 701, 1063LE, Amsterdam (1632). This mill was used for keeping the Osdorperbinnen polder dry. It was used until 1950.

De 1100 Roe, Herman Bonpad 6, 1067SN, Amsterdam (1674). This mill was also used to keep a polder dry.

It was close to the previous one until 1965, when it was moved since it was no longer used.

D'Admiraal, Noordhollandschkanaaldijk 21, 1034ZL, Amsterdam (1792). This mill was used for crushing stone, such as chalk or tufa. It was used till 1954. Restored in 1967, it still turns from time to time.

De Riekermolen, De Borcht 10, 1083AC Amsterdam (1636). This mill, situated alongside the River Amstel, is still in use to keep the Buitenveldert area dry and is supported by electric pumps.

De Gooyer, Funenkade 5, 1018AL, Amsterdam (18th c.).

We do not know the precise date of construction of this mill, which has only been in its current location since 1814.

It is the highest mill in The Netherlands and was used for milling grain.

It's particularly well known because of the small restaurant nearby.

THE DE OTTER MILL ⑯

De Otter, Gillis van Ledenberchstraat 78, 1052VK Amsterdam

One of the five last "paltrok" mills in The Netherlands

Amsterdam still has eight windmills, which, with the galloping development of the town, are becoming more and more hidden and, unfortunately, often lack enough wind to make them turn. The De Otter mill, even though it recently ceased to be operational, still adds a certain charm to the district.

The development of sawmills dates from the beginning of the 17th century. This is partly explained by the breaking up of the Guild of Wood-Sawyers in 1627, which ended their monopoly, but also by considerable technical developments. Around 1590, Cornelis Cornelisz. designed the "paltrok" mill. This is a type of post-mill. The whole structure turns around a post, to turn the sails towards the wind. The name "paltrok" comes from the shape of a long full jacket worn by men at that time. The mill, being low with a wide base, facilitated the handling of timber.

On 18 June 1631, the "Zaagmolencompagnie" (Sawmills Company) was founded. A dozen mills were built just to the west of the Amsterdam ramparts in response to the demand for timber for the shipyards and for construction in general, especially for piles. By the middle of the 18th century, there were almost 40 sawmills in Amsterdam, and more than 80 at the beginning of the 19th century. "De Otter" is the last of the 12 mills constructed in 1631. It is quite small, measuring only 19 metres high. The space inside is so limited that only two or three people can enter at one time, by a ladder. Conceived for sawing beams, it was restored in 1996 and has been classed as a historical monument since 2006. It's the oldest "paltrok" mill in The Netherlands.

There is talk of moving it to Uitgeest, where Cornelis Cornelisz. built his first "paltrok" mill in 1592.

In the 17th century, in the region of Amsterdam, mills had two main uses: managing the water level, by means of an endless screw which enabled the water to be raised from the polders, and sawing timber to satisfy the needs of economic development.

TO SEE NEARBY

THE MAN WITH THE VIOLIN

At the crossing of Tweede Marnixplantsoen and Marnixsraat,
1015ZP Amsterdam

On this square, on a low wall, stands an anonymous steel sculpture. Dating from 1982, it represents a headless man carrying a violin case, hat in hand. It's been said that he's rushing to catch the No 10 tram!

THE BUILDING OF THE COMPANIONS

Bilderdijkstraat 42-44, 1052NB Amsterdam

This building takes its name from two series of four ceramic pictures, each depicting different crafts. On the left, at No 44, one can recognize the black-smith, the glazier, the electrician and the architect. On the right, at No 42, one can see the wallpaper hanger, the painter, the builder and the joiner.

THE CHILDREN'S SWIMMING POOL

Frederik Hendrikstraat 105, 1052HZ Amsterdam

Swimming lessons are an integral part of education in The Netherlands and knowing how to swim is an essential means to survive. Lessons in this former pool only lasted for twenty minutes, hence its nickname "Commando Pool". This building was constructed in 1901 by Hendrik Leguyt and is now turned into apartments. Its surprising chalet style adds an amusing touch to the area.

THE PYRAMIDS

Jan van Galenstraat, 1051KM Amsterdam

In the early 1980s, on the north of Marcanti Island, the Soeters van Eldonk architectural firm conceived a very original building which consists of two triangular shaped towers, in the image of the shape of the island, merging into each other. They contain 82 dwellings.

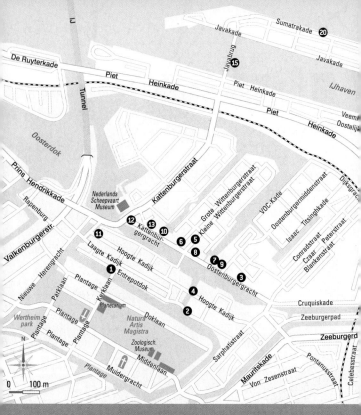

THE NORTHEASTERN

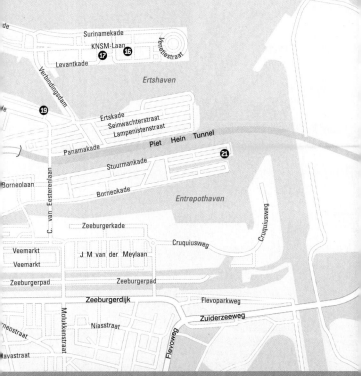

ISLES DISTRICT

THE WALL OF THE WAREHOUSES (ENTREPOTS) ❶

At the level of Entrepotdok 36, 1018AD Amsterdam

> *A witness of the Napoleonic era*

Behind the great bonded warehouses of the Entrepotdok, which were rehabilitated as dwellings at the beginning of the 20th century, a low wall reminds visitors of the history of this place.

The development of commercial activity, already well developed on the east side of the port, accelerated at the beginning of the 19th century. During the period of the Napoleonic occupation, the system of customs duties was modified. Only merchandise destined for The Netherlands was taxed, while goods in transit were not. Since warehouses were scattered about the town at the time, inspection was difficult and trafficking was impossible to control.

Specific warehouses were therefore constructed in two phases. Between 1827 and 1830, 84 great buildings were conceived by architect J. de Greef on the former Rapenburgergracht, renamed with the French word "entrepôt". These buildings were named after 84 large commercial towns in The Netherlands and Flanders, in alphabetical order. Thus, storage of bonded goods was gradually brought together into the same area and a surrounding wall was built to protect against theft. Entry was through a door situated on the current Rapenburgerplein. The great wall ran round behind the buildings towards what is today the Laagte Kadijk (see page 292). This free zone system lasted until 1895. Then transformed into dwellings, these former "entrepôts" have retained their fine façades. Numerous passages have been created to get to the rear of the buildings where you can still see the surrounding wall, which has been reduced to a much lower height.

TO SEE NEARBY

THE CALENDAR WAREHOUSE (ENTREPOT) ❷
Kalenderpanden, Entrepotdok 87-98, 1018AD Amsterdam

In the extension of the first series of warehouses, there is a second, very long "entrepôt" composed of 12 buildings named after the months of the year, whence the name "the calendar buildings". They were built between 1837 and 1840 by architect C.W.M. Klijn to increase the storage capacity for merchandise in transit.

This line of "entrepôts" is 800 metres long. They were squatted by artists from 1996 and their evacuation led to numerous protests. Nevertheless, they were completely rehabilitated in 2001 and are worth a look to see the architectural achievement at the rear.

The architect Joop van Stigt has retained the façade while creating a very large, private garden and the rear façade seems to float like a stage set.

THE WERKSPOOR INDUSTRIAL MUSEUM ❸

Werkspoor museum
Oostenburgergracht 77, 1018NC Amsterdam
• Visit by appointment by phoning 020 625 10 35
• Entry charge

A witness to the Industrial Revolution

Only to be visited by appointment, the Werkspoor Industrial Museum traces the history of the technical creativity of an industrial company, specializing in the mechanical field, from the 19th century on.

This epic story starts in 1826, the year when Paul van Vlissingen started a forge and repair shop for the steam engines of the "Amsterdamse Stoombootmaatschappij", an Amsterdam steam boat company. It was the beginning of the industrial revolution. Van Vlissingen received the support of King William I, who was in exile in England during the Napoleonic occupation. The King, having witnessed the explosion of industry there, wanted to help The Netherlands develop its own industrial base.

In 1848, the company developed its own steam locomotives. By 1850, more than 1000 employees were working on steam engines for use in ships, the sugar industry or railways. The name Werkspoor (railway works) began to be used about 1890 and, in 1929, it became the company's official name. In 1954, however, after its merger with the Stork company, it became the VMF (Verenigde Machinefabrieken: Associated Machine Builders).

After further mergers, the remaining industrial activities, linked to aeronautics and aerospace, were transferred to the town of Hengelo. Today, on the ground floor of the museum, paintings and furniture linked to the V.O.C. period are displayed. On the first floor, the accent is on the industrial heritage.

There, one can find scale models of trains, engines and other Werkspoor industrial products from the 19th and 20th centuries. One can also see works by Herman Heyenbrock, a painter who specialised in industrial scenes.

The Werkspoor museum is situated in a building dating from 1660 called "lijnbaan", meaning "ropewalk", and which was used by the V.O.C. (see page 51). The long narrow ground it occupies, about 500 metres long, was used for making ropes for ships. At each end of the area was a wheel which enabled the long strands of hemp to be twisted several times in the production of thick ropes that were strong in tension.

THE SHIP ENGINE MUSEUM
4

Werfmuseum 't Kromhout• Hoogte Kadijk 147, 1018BJ Amsterdam
• Tel.: 020 627 67 77 • Open Tuesdays 10am-3pm • Entry charge

The little ship engine museum is located in the oldest shipyard still in operation. Traces can be found showing that the land was bought back in 1757. The museum presents numerous exhibits and models explaining how they worked. Even if old engines don't inspire you, you'll doubtless enjoy the timeless ambiance created by the two great metal sheds covering the ramps down which ships slid back into the water after repair. The name Kromhout is that of a brand of engines that enjoyed a very high reputation in Dutch nautical circles.

THE STONES OF THE DAM AND THE WITTENBURGERPLEIN
5

Wittenburgerplein, 1018KK Amsterdam

On Wittenburger Square, behind the East Church (Oosterkerk), the artists Scorselo and Swart have produced a work of art entitled "Moving the World", using stones brought from eight cities in the world: Ankara, Antwerp, Athens, Cairo, Casablanca, Jakarta, Copenhagen and Oslo. This work, which is intended to symbolise understanding between different cultures, originates in the renovation of the Dam Square in 2004. Following the work, a lot of paving stones remained unused and these two artists had the idea of exchanging them for paving stones from other cities around the world. They used them to create a great star with eight points, each of which is paved with stones of a different shape and colour. The star is embedded in a great circle representing the world.

PLAQUE COMMEMORATING THE WINTER FAMINE OF 1944
6

On the East Church (1671), Kleine Wittenburgerstraat 1,
1018LS Amsterdam • Tel.: 020 627 22 80

The protestant East Church was built in 1699 by architect Daniel Stalpert. On the façade to the right of the entry door is a stone carving, commemorating the 1944 famine, by Hildo Krop, a well-known sculptor of the Amsterdam School (see page 270). On it, one can see a mother with her

two children watching a passing boat. During the great famine of the winter of 1944, numerous churches distributed foodstuffs offered by the inhabitants of the north of the country, particularly Friesland. The text inscribed on the plaque recalls the gratitude of the inhabitants of this district towards those who saved them from starving to death.

TO SEE NEARBY

THE STATUE OF TWO MEN SPINNING A ROPE ❼
Oostenburgergracht 37, 1018NB Amsterdam

At the junction of Oostenburgergracht and Oostenburgervoorstraat is a bronze statue representing two young men in a pose that could seem incongruous to passers-by. They are, in fact, in the act of twisting a rope, a symbol of the craft that was practised on a team basis, in this area, in the 17th century (see page 287).

THE HOUSE OF AAT VELDHOEN ❽
Wittenburgergracht 239-241, 1018MX Amsterdam

The house of the painter Aat Veldhoen can be recognized by the great palette of colours that adorns the façade, and by the stone carving representing a painter standing with his palette in front of his easel and his nude model. Do not miss the door handle.

THE COPY OF THE JUDGEMENT OF SOLOMON ❾
Oostenburgergracht 37, 1018NB Amsterdam

You need to look past the garish colours of the ground-floor pizzeria and look high up on this lovely house at No 37 Ooostenburgergracht to see a high-relief depicting the Judgement of Solomon, carved by the sculptor Quellinus in the 17th century for the Palace of Justice on the Dam. The scene represents Solomon casting judgement on two women, each of whom claimed to be the mother of an infant. Solomon threatened to kill the child so as not to be deceived by either of them. The one who responded by asking Solomon to spare the child, thus giving it to the other woman, showed, by this surge of affection, the credibility of her claim to maternity.

THE REMAINS OF ST MARY'S GROTTO ❿
Wittenburgergracht 77-95,
1018MX Amsterdam

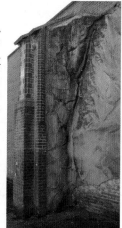

In the middle of Wittenburgergracht Avenue, between the houses, a wide corridor leads to a canal. Apart from the charm of this spot, its two ends have retained the remnants of a former rich religious life. First, go to the end of the corridor and take several steps to the right to see the remains of St Mary's Grotto (Mariagrot). On these ruins, architect P. J. Bekkers built a new church in 1899 whose walls stand on the stones of the grotto. The secret church of St Anne, which had occupied a building on Prins Hendrikkade since 1720, was moved to this new building, but it was closed in 1970, then demolished in 1978 to make way for social housing. However, the ceiling in the corridor is retained, as was the façade pediment, where one can read "R K vd Hanna" (Roman Catholic St Anne), and the attractive wrought iron grill with a golden cross in the centre.

TO SEE NEARBY

THE STATUE OF A SAILOR
Kadijkplein 17-18, 1018AC Amsterdam

Produced in 1980 by Joost Barbiers, the statue situated at Nos 17-18 Kadijkplein represents a stylised sailor, recognisable by his fisherman's hat. It recalls the presence of sailors in this area and particularly in the big building called "Zeemanshuis" (Sailors' House) situated here.

Built in 1858 by A. N. Godefroy, it overlooked the Valkenstijn naval yard at the time. Sailors who were waiting for their ships to be repaired were lodged here.

THE FALSE FAÇADES OF KATTENBURGERPLEIN ⑫
Kattenburgerplein, 1018KK Amsterdam

Although the very attractive Kattenburgerplein looks as if it has remained unchanged since the 17th century, in reality it is a complete reconstruction from the 1970s. The isles of Kattenburg, Wittenburg and Oostenburg were created between 1653 and 1658 in the River IJ. They were intended to protect the town in case of conflict, as The Netherlands had already experienced numerous wars against Spain, England and France.

Over the years, their military usefulness diminished to give place to economic activity linked to the shipyards. Thus, numerous houses were built for the shipyard workers. Very few have been preserved, but, in 1968, architect Pieter Pals decided to give new life to some of these houses by using what was left to create a new complex of student housing on Kattenburg Place. As surprising as it may appear, these lovely façades are artificial. One door out of two does not open! Note also the attractive "de Groenne Ovent" façade stone representing a baker putting bread into a green-coloured oven.

THE TRUE OLD HOUSES ⑬
Kattenburgergracht 7-17, 1018KN Amsterdam

The houses at No 7-17 Kattenburgergracht are the only ones to have survived from the origins of the Isle of Kattenburg. They date from the second half of the 17th century. At No 9, note the gable stone representing a basket of nails. Ironmonger Willem Claeszoon lived in this house.

Higher on the façade one can read the year it was built. The houses at Nos 11, 13 and 15 were also built in 1663. The gable stone representing two pulleys indicates that a joiner who specialised in ship's timber work laboured here.

On Kattenburger Place stands a bronze statue produced in 1968 by Alphonse Freimuth. This statue, called "The Navigator", symbolises the link between this area and the world of sailing ships.

"Kadijk" means summer dyke or interior dyke. Built from the 13th century, these dykes protected the town from being taken by storm by waves from the sea. Rembrandt immortalised the landscapes created around these dykes in numerous paintings and engravings.

THE HOUSES OF THE "YOUNG HEROES" ⓮

Brantasgracht, Lamonggracht, Majanggracht
and Seranggracht, 1019 Amsterdam

Have confidence in the Young

While the town plan for the Isle of Java was developed by architect Sjoerd Soeters, the planning for the four cross canals was entrusted to 19 young architects, nicknamed "The young heroes". The best known were Rene van Zuuk, designer of the ARCAM building, and Bjarne Mastenbroek, who was known for the De Postbank tea pavilion in the Hoge Veluwe Park. Each designed two houses, all with the same dimensions (4.5m x 16m x 9m) and with a garden behind, to create a modern version of the 17th-century houses found around the grand canals. The design of each house is repeated four times, as the houses on the two first and last canals are the same, and along each canal the houses on one side mirror those on the other. However, the inhabitants have reduced the symmetry here and there by changing the paint colours. The names of the canals represent those of rivers, towns and islands of current day Indonesia, with which the KNSM company (see below) maintained links.

TO SEE NEARBY

THE JAN SCHAEFER BRIDGE, CALLED THE LIZARD ⓯
The Oostelijke Handelskade, going towards Java Island

This big, 200 metre-long bridge was built in 2001 to connect the eastern part of the town to Java Island. Designed by architect Ton Venhoeven, the Jan Schaefer Bridge actually comprises three bridges, separating the traffic of pedestrians, cyclists and motorists. Its asymmetrical form is a rather futuristic composition whose shape reminds one of a lizard, whence its nickname. In the initial town plan, the bridge was to have been the extension of a new highway direct from the town centre to the harbour. The De Zwijger warehouse wasn't going to be retained, but once it was classified as a historical monument, it had to be integrated into the urban architecture. That is why one has to pass through a tunnel beneath the warehouse to get to the bridge, creating a clean break between the architecture of the town centre and that of the port. The bridge gets its name from town councillor Jan Schaefer well known for his work on social housing in Amsterdam. It is rather ironic that a bridge leading to one of the new smart areas of town should be named after this defender of social programmes.

The KNSM Island was created in 1896 by extending Java Island. Like the latter, it acted as a breakwater to protect the town from the waves of the Zuider Zee before it became a lake. It takes its name from the Koninklijke Nederlandsche Stoomboot Maatschappij (Royal Netherlands Steamship Company), a line which provided shipping links with Surinam and the Levant.

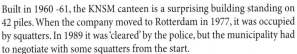

THE KNSM CANTEEN ARTISTS' WORKSHOPS   **16**
KSNM-kantine, KNSM-laan 1019LK Amsterdam

Built in 1960 -61, the KNSM canteen is a surprising building standing on 42 piles. When the company moved to Rotterdam in 1977, it was occupied by squatters. In 1989 it was 'cleared' by the police, but the municipality had to negotiate with some squatters from the start.

Thus, some squatters were able to become proprietors of the canteen for a symbolic price of 0.50€. In 2000, one of the former squatters sold his share in the canteen for 500,000 Euros.

THE NUTS OF THE PIREUS BUILDING PILLARS   **17**
Between KNSM-laan and Levantkade, 1019LK Amsterdam

The East side of the Pireus building stands on 24 cylindrical pillars, each composed of five sections joined together by giant nuts. These pillars, created in 1995, are the work of Arno van den Mark and are called the Pireus Passage, as it provides a passage between the street and the water. On each of the 96 nuts is a reproduction of part of the map of the city of Paris, into which the artist has inserted photos of monuments, famous people or streets, symbolising a sort of look back to the past. One can easily find the Opera, Trocadero or Montparnasse. These little maps are lit up at night.

TO SEE NEARBY

WORK OF ART CALLED "FOR THE BEES"

At the junction of Panamalaan and Fred Petterbaan,
Tram stop Rietlanden, 1019JT Amsterdam

Frank Mandersloot worked on "For the Bees" for 9 years. Unveiled in 2004, this artwork measures 16 meters high and represents three tables on top of one another. The one at the bottom is in concrete while the two at the top are made of exotic hardwood. These tables symbolise the town of Amsterdam, which is built on piles, as well as the different levels of organisation of public spaces – tramways, cycle paths and roads. Beneath the tables, there used to be several swarms of bees housed in eight hives and managed by bee-keepers. While the bees have not survived, the work of art has been named after them.

THE HAMMOCKS OF THE RUSSIAN CARGO SHIP "ODESSA"

Veemkade 259, 1019CZ Amsterdam • Tel.: 020 419 30 10
• Open Wednesday, Thursday and Sunday from 4pm to 1am,
Saturday to 3am

Odessa is a replica of a Russian cargo ship from the 1920s that is anchored in the port of Amsterdam to the east of Centraal Station, beside the bridge leading to KNSM Island. In summer, you are warmly welcomed for lunch and you can relax in a sailor's hammock on the bridge of the ship to enjoy a superb view of the old port.

COMPASS ISLAND

Kompas Eiland, visible from Sumatrakadeon Java eiland

Compass Island is a tiny island on a sandbank in the river IJ, to the north of Java Island. In former times, sailors used this island as an orientation point to align their maritime compasses. In the 1990s, a project involving a 20-hectare extension of the island, in order to build 400 dwellings, was started. The project was dropped, however, allowing this island to keep its old-fashioned charm.

THE TREE OF THE HOUSE AT NO 120 SCHEEPSTIMMERMANSTRAAT ㉑

Scheepstimmermanstraat 120, 1019WZ Amsterdam

> *The most surprising house on Borneo Island*

Among the modern constructions of Borneo Island, don't miss seeing the surprising houses on Scheepstimmermanstraat. They are particularly nice to see from the canal side, by going up and down Stokerkade Quay. They are like a portfolio on the expertise of the best Dutch architectural practices.

On this small part of the island, the town did not refer to major construction companies, but gave 60 individuals the opportunity to undertake their own projects. For the first time since the 17th century, the town of Amsterdam actually sold building plots to private individuals.

The freedom of design was very constrained, however, since each house had to comply with certain precise dimensions: a total height not exceeding 9.2m, which included 3.5m for the ground floor. The result is an interesting mosaic of styles and materials.

The situation of the houses located between the street and the quay is also interesting, as their design had to respond to two levels, the street being higher than the quay. So, on the street side, they have at least one parking space, sometimes two, thanks to an ingenious lift system, as at numbers 44 and 66. On the quay side, they sometimes have a garage for the boat.

The most original house is certainly the one at number 120. Architect Koen van Velsen built it. The surprise comes from the tall acacia tree growing from the hallway on the ground floor, through the levels of the house, and up to the glass roof, reaching more than 10 meters high. At the first floor level, some branches have been sawn off to form a small seat. At the top floor level, the tree becomes a piece of decoration. Only a glass panel separates the living room from the tree.

The roof has openings to let rainwater through. The tree, which grows so fast that its branches push up through these holes, was planted in a concrete container so that the roots cannot damage the foundations. In spring, the tree's white flowers give off a honey-like perfume. The deciduous foliage provides protection from the sun in summertime, but lets in light in the winter.

At the junction of Panamalaan and Rietlandpark, in 2002, architect Rudy Uytenhaak built a group of buildings called "Hoop, Liefde en Fortuin" (Hope, Love and Luck), recalling the name of three sawmills which were located there in the 19th century.

UNUSUAL HOTELS
IN AMSTERDAM

◀ ## LLOYD HOTEL ❶
TWO BEDS FOR SEVEN PEOPLE
Oostelijke Handelskade 34, 1019BN Amsterdam • www.lloydhotel.com
• From 220€ for these two rooms

This big building situated on the docks in the eastern part of the city has a rich and unconventional history. Built to accommodate immigrants en route to America, it was used during the war as a holding point for Jews, before later housing artist studios. Recently transformed into a hotel-restaurant by the best Dutch designers, it offers 1-to-5-star rooms at all price levels. Two rooms (of which one has a grand piano) have a bed for seven people. It is strongly recommended to use the entire capacity of these beds. For just two people to use them is a real waste.

THE ST CHRISTOPHER'S HOTEL AT THE WINSTON ❷
THE RESULT OF AN ANNUAL DESIGN COMPETITION
Warmoesstraat 129-131, 1012JA Amsterdam • www.st-christophers.co.uk
• 44€ for two people

Each room of this low-cost hotel in the city centre was designed by the winner of an annual design contest organised by Aldert Mantje and Andre Mesman, the then creative directors of the hotel.

MAROXIDIEN ❸
SLEEP IN A "WOONBOOT"
Prins Hendrikkade 534, 1011TE Amsterdam • www.lemaroxidien.com/
• Tel.:020 400 4006
• 110€ for two people

A unique experience -- sleeping on an old barge on the canals of Amsterdam like one of the many inhabitants who have chosen this kind of habitation.

DE WINDKETEL ❹
A NIGHT IN A PUMPING STATION
Watertorenplein 8-C, 1051PA Amsterdam • www.windketel.nl/
• 300€ for two people for two nights

Only 15 minutes from the Jordaan, this attractive little octagonal building is three levels high. It was part of the Amsterdam pumping station complex and has been transformed into a charming guesthouse.

THE LUTE SUITES ❺
Amsteldijk Zuid 54-58, 1184VD Ouderkerk a/d Amstel • Tel.: 020-47 22 462
• 285€ for a twin bedded room including breakfast

A few kilometres away from Amsterdam, in the lovely village of Ouderkerk on the river Amstel, Peter Lute, famous for his Amsterdam restaurant, opened seven guestrooms in small houses aligned along the riverside. They were part of an old 18th-century gunpowder factory. The rooms have been renovated in an innovative way by the famous designer Marcel Wanders.

ALPHABETICAL INDEX

ALPHABETICAL INDEX

ALPHABETICAL INDEX

THEMATIC INDEX

AMSTERDAM WATER

ARCHITECTURE

ART, MUSIC AND PAINTING

BARS AND RESTAURANTS

THEMATIC INDEX

HEBRAISM

HISTORY

HOFJES AND GARDENS

THEMATIC INDEX

INDUSTRIAL HERITAGE

LITTLE KNOWN MUSEUMS

RELIGION AND THE ESOTERIC

THE AMSTERDAM SCHOOL

UNUSUAL HOTELS IN AMSTERDAM

Acknowledgements:
Our warmest thanks to Christelle de Cazenove for her contribution as well as to Ken Maxfield for his editing, Minne Dijkstra for his historical comments and Victoria de Regt for her support. We would also like to thank the Tesselschade Arbeid Adelt Association for its hospitality. Special thanks to Guy Roberts and Christa Roberts-van Eys for the English translation.

Photography credits:
All photos were taken by Lynn Van der Velden except for:
Thomas Jonglez (cover)
Herman van Iperen (photo of the Tramway Museum – Zidouta on Flickr)
Museum Speelklok (photo of the Barrel Organ Museum)
Thomas Mayer (photo of the Occohofje)
Artis Zoo (photo of the aquarium)
Jona Andersen (photo of the Berlage Citadel)
Alexander van Eys (photos from the wall of the warehouses and the R.E.M. island)
Vereniging Vrienden van Amsterdamse Gevelstenen (photos of the gable stones)

Maps: Jean-Baptiste Neny
Lay-out Design: Roland Deloi
Lay-out: Françoise Natan
Translation: Guy Roberts
Editing: Kimberly Bess
Cover: Romaine Guérin

© JONGLEZ 2012

June 2012 – Edition 02
ISBN: 978-2-36195-022-4

Printed in France